"*elseship* is a kaleidoscopic exploration of all that can exist between two people caught between friendship and unrequited love. It's a gorgeous and delicately rendered tapestry of desires—and a bracing examination of what happens when feelings break the boxes and labels meant to neatly contain them."

—Angela Chen, author of *Ace: What Asexuality Reveals About Desire, Society, and the Meaning of Sex*

"Nothing triggers archival fervor quite like unrequited love. For those of us who have ever Googled 'what is love' late into the night, this book is ours. Tree Abraham has managed to do the impossible: transform the excesses of that delirious, excruciating fever state into a true work of art." —Anelise Chen, author of *So Many Olympic Exertions*

elseship

: an unrequited affair

tree abraham

SOFT SKULL   NEW YORK

elseship: an unrequited affair

First Soft Skull edition: 2025

Grateful acknowledgment for reprinting materials is made to the following: "On Subtlety," copyright © 2018 by Meghan O'Gieblyn. Reprinted by permission of the Frances Goldin Literary Agency.

Library of Congress Cataloging-in-Publication Data
Names: Abraham, Tree, author.
Title: Elseship : an unrequited affair / Tree Abraham.
Description: First Soft Skull edition. | New York : Soft Skull, 2025. | Includes bibliographical references.
Identifiers: LCCN 2024037981 | ISBN 9781593767853 (trade paperback) | ISBN 9781593767860 (ebook)
Subjects: LCSH: Abraham, Tree—Friends and associates. | Authors, Canadian—21st century—Biography. | Sexual minorities—Biography. | Unrequited love. | Friendship. | LCGFT: Autobiographies.
Classification: LCC PR9199.4.A2344 Z46 2025 | DDC 818/.6 [B]—dc23/eng/20240830
LC record available at https://lccn.loc.gov/2024037981

Art and book design by Tree Abraham

Soft Skull Press
New York, NY
www.softskull.com

Printed in the United States of America

1 3 5 7 9 10 8 6 4 2

For M

I think about a particular individual, perhaps a rare bird, one who has been exiled for documenting facts and archiving flight patterns and creating maps and observing different species of trees, this bird who sees value in concretizing memory to outlast one's own life and trajectory. This bird is also capable of being homesick, of longing for a home that exists or could one day exist, because language, diagrammed and phantomized and stricken, is also capable of forging a threshold between this world and the dream world, and so that in-betweenness might be construed as a concrete space, and there might be new language vociferated to articulate all that does not yet fit into the confines of the current restrictions of what is *known*.

—JANICE LEE

what were they anyway, sprigs of grass, things of blue?
For a long time I wanted to use words, then didn't
—MARY RUEFLE

In that first year after my admission of love, there were starts and stops transitioning from being housemates and friends into an undefined elseship. A few days after my birthday, I was lying on the couch dripping heartache inchoate of my soon-to-be unrequited love, you were sitting next to me stroking my hair. This was the last time it would be simple, you illimitably unfiltered, us a weightless relation. I couldn't have known it then, how we would be redefined in a moment like nothing had come before and tomorrow would never arrive. All at once our loose grains of sand hardened into a glassy mass, and that year, and all of our years in relation to one another thereafter, would forever remain a conundrum of flash and rock.

We had hard talks every few months after that. About how we struggled to trust each other, the ways it made us writhe. Thrumming, spasming, the question that nagged in us: Were we allowed to exist?

One such talk happened on New Year's Eve, almost a year after the admission. You said, Maybe this talk was what we needed to reset. *As the clock approached and passed midnight, I lay on the couch and you sat next to me stroking my hair for the first time since that last time. Then you lay your head on me, and I stroked your hair for the first time, and you fell asleep and so did I. In a way, this end to that year felt like a reset, but in truth, we were somewhere entirely new. This is an account of our in-between, because that is where we live, that is where our love was found.*

The story of you and me starts where most end: unrequited love confronting friendship.

Here is written many things about us. So many specific things that it might appear to include everything. It does not. It does not include your side. Everything written here is what psychologists term *myside bias*.

It leaves out things I love and dislove about you that are too personal.
It leaves out moments that tasted so sweet but melted too fast.
It excludes some of the worst acts that transpired between us
that need not be recapitulated.
And only includes your words when possible to directly transcribe.
Written here are nonchronological snapshots compressing and
shuffling time and void.

To pin this book to dates would imply that love remains loyal to days both in arrangement and duration. But love, and memory, are unconcerned with locating themselves. They are forces. Though I tried to keep this book in that first year, some realities and insights slip in from beyond it—to the equally challenging years that followed where we stayed living together, then when we didn't—but mostly, while we kept going, my revelations and observations of our dynamic hold true to what took place in year one, even if I've had to relearn them again and again in nonlinear order.

This book cannot contain everything because it is a book, not a life. Or so I told myself. I must not live in this book. Once recorded, I should abandon what is not written and move beyond it, back into an unwritten future. But we are storytellers, constantly gathering fragmented happenings into a recognizable shape, making choices about how to interpret hardships and windfalls. The stories we tell ourselves about who we are and how we came to be forge our identities. My gut is a jumble of fear-filled hysterias. I fear that love and happy and all good things might be like fisting a handful of sand, with grains trickling out every second until the palm is dusted with grit but mostly left gripping itself.

To endure our complexity, I had to actively solder **facets** of us into a meaningful narrative.

That year I needed this story, I still do.

Each time I've tried to sequence the story, it has resisted arborescence, I am not the tree I was when I began telling it. I kept changing and so did everything between us. Deleuze and Guattari write about how the romantic structure of a book is dialectic to nature, hierarchical, and with a binary logic that betrays the intricacy of life. They propose a counter-structure, with *rhizomes* and *lines of flight*: no subject or object, only undifferentiated space and ruptures in predetermined thoughtways. When a paradigm breaks, lines of flight offer entrances toward new intensities, identities, and connections. When a rhizome splinters along old or new nodes, it fractalizes but remains whole.

You see, we started as housemates, soon became friends . . . then I fell in love and you didn't and we kept going, being housemates, being friends, becoming something else. What we'll end as—there isn't a word for that.

In a way, our persistence gave rise to rhizomes. But our unrequited affair also marooned me. What I have done here is tweezed out shards—of definitions, metaphors, memories, moments, feelings—and welded them together along lines of flight, removing and replacing and fusing new and old remnants into a -ship of some sort that I could hold in book form.

facet: one of many definable aspects of something (a situation, subject, object, person's character, etc.); the small sides cut into gemstones to increase light reflection

4

I am a pilgrim peregrinating for words. Those with obscure, exacting definitions that confirm through their existence that a seemingly particular phenomena also belongs to the universal. You know this. I love how sometimes you say, *There should be a word for that*, and I will try to find one, and you are elated if I do.

Believing synonyms did not exist, Gustave Flaubert was in constant search for the most precise "right word" (*le mot juste*) for every occasion. Homer called it a *winged word*. What does a winged word provoke? Perhaps I believe that fashioning a word in the shape of a phenomenon can liberate me from ever again needing language for it, and the new species of word, once spelled out, can immediately fly away.

Some definitions of new and old words encountered this year became glass lenses in a **lighthouse**, straightening the beam seen through the fog of what our -ship meant.

lighthouse: When lighthouses began to use gigantic lenses to strengthen their beams, the glass was solid, heavy, and expensive, with a thickness that weakened the penetrating light. In 1822, physicist and civil engineer Augustin Fresnel invented a new lightweight design of glass lenses that wrap around a lamp to refract scattering light into concentrated parallel beams. The *Fresnel lens* stairsteps hundreds of cut-glass panels into concentric rings, which can radiate an infinite combination of constant or flashing light patterns across great distances.

‹ ‹ ‹ ‹ facet ‹ ‹ ‹ rhizome ‹ ‹ ‹ lines of flight ‹

‹ ‹ ‹ ‹ lighthouse ‹ ‹ ‹ le mot juste ‹ ‹ ‹ winged word ‹ ‹ ‹ ‹ ‹ ‹ ‹ ‹ ‹ ‹ ‹ ‹ ‹ ‹ ‹ ‹ ‹

‹ ‹ ‹ ‹ kilig ‹ ‹ ‹ yuánfèn ‹ ‹ ‹ cafuné ‹

‹ ‹ ‹ ‹ ammil ‹ ‹ ‹ eagle-eyed ‹ ‹ ‹ agape ‹ ‹ ‹ grok ‹ ‹ ‹ ‹ ‹ ‹ ‹ ‹ ‹ ‹ ‹ ‹ ‹ ‹

‹ ‹ ‹ ‹ pigeon ‹ ‹ ‹ photophilic ‹ ‹ ‹ hummingbird ‹ ‹ ‹ ‹ ‹ ‹ ‹ ‹ ‹ ‹ ‹ ‹ ‹ ‹

‹ ‹ ‹ ‹ meniscus ‹ ‹ ‹ philautia ‹ ‹ ‹ xiu chi ‹ ‹ ‹ xiu kui ‹ ‹ ‹ ‹ ‹ ‹ ‹ ‹ ‹ ‹

‹ ‹ ‹ ‹ mudlark ‹ ‹ ‹ haecceity ‹ ‹ ‹ penguin ‹ ‹ ‹ ‹ ‹ ‹ ‹ ‹ ‹ ‹ ‹ ‹ ‹ ‹

‹ ‹ ‹ ‹ block ‹ ‹ ‹ ludus ‹ ‹ ‹ crane ‹ ‹ ‹ ‹ ‹ ‹ ‹ ‹ ‹ ‹ ‹ ‹ ‹ ‹ ‹ ‹ ‹ ‹

‹ ‹ ‹ ‹ glitter ball ‹ ‹ ‹ bowerbird ‹ ‹ ‹ philia ‹ ‹ ‹ ‹ ‹ ‹ ‹ ‹ ‹ ‹ ‹ ‹ ‹

‹ ‹ ‹ ‹ anam cara ‹ ‹ ‹ dingledodies ‹ ‹ ‹ eros ‹ ‹ ‹ ‹ ‹ ‹ ‹ ‹ ‹ ‹ ‹ ‹ ‹

‹ ‹ ‹ ‹ desiderata ‹ ‹ ‹ bittersweet ‹ ‹ ‹ vulgar eros ‹ ‹ ‹ ‹ ‹ ‹ ‹ ‹ ‹

‹ ‹ ‹ ‹ divine eros ‹ ‹ ‹ mania ‹ ‹ ‹ jamais vu ‹ ‹ ‹ ‹ ‹ ‹ ‹ ‹ ‹ ‹

‹ ‹ ‹ ‹ crucible ‹ ‹ ‹ obsession ‹ ‹ ‹ limerence ‹ ‹ ‹ ‹ ‹ ‹ ‹ ‹ ‹

‹ ‹ ‹ ‹ acatalepsy ‹ ‹ ‹ unpunctuated ‹ ‹ ‹ opacity ‹ ‹ ‹ ‹ ‹ ‹ ‹ ‹

‹ ‹ ‹ ‹ pragma ‹ ‹ ‹ grace ‹ ‹ ‹ storge ‹ ‹ ‹ ‹ ‹ ‹ ‹ ‹ ‹ ‹ ‹ ‹ ‹ ‹

‹ ‹ ‹ ‹ hiraeth ‹ ‹ ‹ micromoment ‹ ‹ ‹ fluid mosaic ‹ ‹ ‹ ‹ ‹ ‹ ‹ ‹

‹ ‹ ‹ amatonormativity ‹ ‹ ‹ queer ‹ ‹ ‹ queerplatonic ‹ ‹ ‹ ‹ ‹ ‹ ‹

‹ ‹ ‹ ‹ szeretlek ‹ ‹ ‹ Silly Putty ‹ ‹ ‹ limbic resonance ‹ ‹ ‹ ‹ ‹ ‹ ‹

‹ ‹ ‹ leitmotif ‹ ‹ ‹ extradictionary ‹ ‹ ‹ lethologica ‹ ‹ ‹ ‹ ‹ ‹ ‹

‹ ‹ ‹ ‹ choreography ‹ ‹ ‹ synchrony ‹ ‹ ‹ else ‹ ‹ ‹ ‹ ‹ ‹ ‹ ‹ ‹ ‹

‹ ‹ ‹ ‹ vagus ‹ ‹ ‹ poetic memory ‹ ‹ ‹ amor fati ‹ ‹ ‹ ‹ ‹ ‹ ‹ ‹ ‹ ‹

‹ ‹ ‹ ‹ hypocognition ‹ ‹ ‹ magpie ‹ ‹ ‹ everglow ‹ ‹ ‹ ‹ ‹ ‹ ‹ ‹ ‹ ‹ ‹ ‹

‹ ‹ ‹ ‹ lister ‹ ‹ ‹ Uncertainty Principle ‹ ‹ ‹ butterfly effect ‹ ‹ ‹ ‹ ‹ ‹ ‹ ‹ ‹ ‹

‹ ‹ ‹ ‹ rarae aves ‹ ‹ ‹ unrequited love ‹ ‹ ‹ elseship ‹ ‹ ‹ ‹ ‹ ‹ ‹ ‹ ‹ ‹ ‹ ‹ ‹ ‹ ‹ ‹ ‹ ‹

Words shape stories. We perceive the physical world through language acquired to describe it. We perceive our inner worlds similarly. The more new and specialized words we learn to classify our variegated emotional states, the deeper we are able to delve into ourselves. Language favors the physically observable. The absence of words describing the intangible can limit our ability to define our experiences.

I lap up web listicles of foreign words with no English equivalent, revealing the sensibilities of different cultures. Tagalog's *kilig* is a noun that describes tingling or fluttering felt when overcome with romance. The Mandarin word *yuánfèn* reflects an entire belief system in the fated affinity two people have for one another. *Cafuné* in Portuguese is the verb for running your fingers through a loved one's hair.

I remember the first time you stroked my hair because it was the first time anyone had. You came and sat on my bed one morning while we were talking logistics about our day's field trip. You had overslept. I was fully dressed and wilted over one side of the bed atop freshly laundered sheets, as I waited sleepily for your wake. You perched across from me, apologetic for the delay. Without announcement, your hand reached over to tickle the hair around my ear, as if you had done it a thousand times before. Only a split second of surprise delayed what became an addiction to the sensation. Your small pointy fingers moved like they were playing a string instrument on my scalp. I would have canceled all our plans to stay on the bed like that with your fingers' cradlesong. I couldn't need a word for that feeling before meeting the act that made it. Now I need the winged word because I need the act.

The thing about the word *love* is that it encapsulates a universal feeling but, in every way, feels entirely particular. Never have I felt more common yet, in a moment, unrepeatable. Love heightens everything. It is little things and big things, unusual and plain things, all of it marbleized together.

Carson McCullers wrote a short story about a man trying to teach a boy the ability to love. The man says he made the mistake of starting with the climax of loving a woman, when really he should have started with "A tree. A rock. A cloud."

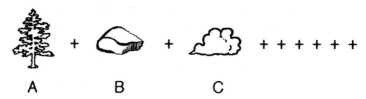

A   B   C

Better to start by loving the small details found in one's surroundings, to find love in every particle that makes up the universe, from which we are inseparable.

Love is granular, also mountainous, enormous—unyielding—a big thing, but it yields, so slow with time, it becomes something else—a Sisyphean boulder, a rolling stone, a rocky road, gravel, sand—little things.

All your things sprinkling over everything like celebratory glitter as I too hover between earth and air. Loving you is *ammil*-like. **Ammil**, the Devon term for the thin film of ice that glazes a landscape after a freeze, every blade of grass to budding twig glimmering in the sunlight.

This icy layer draws me near over and over as you thaw with each re-approach. The slow way in which you reveal yourself compels me to listen intently, to look closer, to really take note and deconstruct the contours and fillings of your person.

I love that you are the goddess of small things. You rest in the subtle, the whispered, the lingering. **Eagle**-eyed, you will read a book on trees then apples then seeds. You know that the infinitesimal gives way to an infinite. That between every line, every letter, every pause lives a sublime truth. That as long as you are curious and patient and still enough, observing a small thing can unlatch a deep knowing of the big things.

It is this quiet, playful delicacy with which you approach everything. A not-too-much, just-enough, lightness of touch.

I am becoming a learned practitioner of this approach through loving you.

—

The love came as a thunderclap on my twenty-eighth birthday.

It is ironic that after years of chasing dynamism in the world's most exotic settings, the wildest trip happened at home.

I had moved in eight months prior, you had already been in the house a year. Each of us four tenants was on a separate month-to-month lease. We were strangers to each other before renting whichever vacant room was being advertised on Craigslist. The landlord let the housemates handle interviewing prospective tenants. The day I came to tour the place, you were not there. I sat with the other two housemates for a friendly chat, benign questions and answers posed on both sides meant to expose larger truths about how we would gel under the same roof. They said you would call me the following day since all three had to approve of

eagle: The expression *eagle-eyed* means to be a keen observer. An eagle's eye is one of the strongest of all animals'—four to eight times stronger than a human's, with a retina fovea of one million cells per square millimeter, compared to 200,000 in humans. Eagles can see more shades and vividness of colors than us and can see ultraviolet light, which means that they can detect bodily traces left by prey.

my suitability. You never called. One of the other housemates emailed soon after and told me the room was mine if I wanted. A week later I was back finalizing paperwork with the landlord when you arrived home, in basic office fashion: black pencil skirt with pale floral top, no hint of a hipster flare donned by myself or peers. You said a polite hello before slipping into your bedroom. The exit felt unnaturally abrupt. I was disappointed we hadn't bonded on the spot. I don't remember thinking much more, or how soon after I hoped to befriend you. We were both busy, used to home being a retreat rather than a social club, so friendship progressed gradually, then, perhaps four months in, exponentially with each encounter. No analysis undertaken, just unspoken mutual pleasure and affection, squarely in the category of friendship. We were becoming a kind of cursive—characters unspooling in a loopy flow, easy and onward.

Before my birthday, it never crossed my mind that I would want more.

———————————— $DAY\ 1$ ————————————

My birthday was on a Wednesday. I suggested a no-fuss evening of takeout with whichever housemates were around since we were hosting a party that weekend for all of our respective friends, under a loose guise of my birthday minus special attention. I came home from an after-work swim to your refulgent face at the door ushering me upstairs to wait until summoned. When I descended, my housemates were sitting in the dining room. The chandelier was dimmed, festooned with mint-green and blue ribbons matching the candles ablaze underneath. Turquoise garland hung against the navy wall, and multicolored tinsel and confetti bespeckled the table set for lasagna and cake. You alone had left work early to decorate and bake. You never left early. A fib about a pipe bursting at the house. The homemade cake was made more impressive by the fact that up until then, the kitchen was without bakeware. The cake had required pans, an electric mixer, foresight.

My entire body was immediately awash with paresthesia. I was vibrating, teary-eyed, and too nauseous to eat. Everyone was touched by how overwhelmed I seemed. But that wasn't it. At the center of my foggy spin were your MoonPie eyes. I felt a desperate desire to express a gratitude in a manner that words would not withstand. Like I wanted to swallow you and the entire thaumaturgic universe that surrounded us and never throw it up. An impossibility that wrenches.

─────────────── DAY 2 ───────────────

I felt this way through the evening and into the next day while sitting in my office cubicle. The pressure was so intense I reached for a notebook to trace the feeling back to its source. At the end of the entry, I googled "lovesickness," accurately diagnosing myself without ever having had an approximate feeling, never having been even fractionally lovesick. Whatever had been called a *crush* in the past was always in a cerebral space. This was chemical intoxication.

In these first gulps of love, I swallowed heartbreak. love. bittersweet. I knew you were too desirous of partnering with a man to want partnership from me (however dated an assessment this seems now). I had also grown accustomed to ambiguous rejection from every crush over the years. My journal entry was already filled with future dismay. Would I ever fall in love like this again, being that it depended on the gradual proximity to someone in my home?

The lovesickness did not subside, not all day, not through every attempt to eat, not during my evening swim. You had after-work things. We didn't see each other that night.

There was a friend that I saw a few times a year when we were in our early twenties, when our travels intersected in different countries. He felt like the greatest potential for love and partnership. I eventually told him that I like-liked him. He didn't feel the same. I was angry, not comprehending how I wasn't enough. I ended the friendship. This kind of rejection taught me to accept the friend zone as the only zone.

I wanted to preemptively combat bitterness before it crept in between us. Know the love was real, even if it was only one-sided. Before bed, I wrote out a list of everything I loved about you. I stopped writing at item 132.

DAY 3

I journaled more. I messaged my somewhat-estranged childhood best friend, A███. "Maybe too personal or weird a question, but remember long ago how you mentioned that you felt like you were in love with K███[our mutual high school best friend]?" We had never spoken about it. I hadn't understood its gravity enough to delve deeper. She of course remembered. She and K███ had remained best friends, they still lived together, like sisters now, she said. A███ told me the feelings eventually faded, helped by falling in love with other people, but it took time because they stayed friends.

After work I met up with a former coworker who had fallen in love with our other, then straight-identifying and coupled, coworker. They were now together, in crazy love. They encouraged me to tell you, that I shouldn't presume how you felt or could feel.

DAY 4

I spent the morning in the corner farthest from my bedroom door curled up on the floor. Sobbing to my mother, calling a close friend, confessing to anyone who was not you. By midday I made my way downstairs to lie on the couch and attempt a meek fact-finding mission. You joined me, stroking my hair as we spoke. You were aware of my melancholic few days. I asked, "Would we be friends if we didn't live together?" You emphatically said, *Yes, of course.* "Does it make you uncomfortable when I say 'I love you'?" *No, I don't say it back because it would be disingenuous to say it only when prompted.* We spent the rest of the day together running errands and setting up for the house party.

Later that night at the party, you confronted me in the kitchen. Alcohol makes you talk more freely. You wanted to revise your comments from earlier in the day. You said that you didn't feel as strongly about our friendship as I did, not yet. *I see the potential for that as we share more experiences and memories over time* . . . I don't remember what else was said, I had never had a conversation about friendship intentions. Why were you doing this now? I hadn't been drinking, but it felt like I had been kicked over sideways.

—————————— DAY 5 ——————————

I confided in more long-distance friends. I read many articles with headlines like "The Science of Romantic Rejection," "Frustration Attraction," "The Neuroscience of Infatuation," "The Neurobiology of a Break-Up," "Unrequited Love in Friendships," "Limerence and Emotional Attachment," "Pain of Unrequited Love Afflicts Rejecter, Too." There was no comfort to be found in these external truths. I wished to not be in my life.

—————————— DAY 6 ——————————

Monday comes. The physical symptoms still raging. It takes all my strength to dress, commute to work, sit at my desk, and look like I am designing instead of stuck in a loop, journaling the same feelings as the prior pages. There is no tantrum over the wounding injustice of unrequited love. The love is bound up small and frozen as the shock of lovesickness launches me into damage control. I am consciously yearning to steer into acceptance, to a scenario that minimizes animosity and alleviates this chilling darkness, like I am in a cave mining for hope.

—————————— DAY 7 ——————————

I usually tackle emotions as they arise, researching and processing with friends and problem-solving my way back to a peace. But my brainy tactics weren't working to dampen my bodily distress. I was devolving further into wreckage without resolve. We lived together. *We live together.* I didn't know what this love would do to me or for how long.

That evening you came home and asked if I wanted to talk about my melancholy, still evidenced in my anguished expression. *You don't have to if you're not ready, but I think I know what it's about.*

I had to tell you.

The words of that conversation did not embed in me. My memory of it is out-of-body and behind glass. We sat at a distance on my bedroom floor. My voice shaking, my eyes apologetic. Your voice solicitous, your eyes sodden.

I told you.
You already knew.
You had caused lovesickness many times before.

Telling you changed everything, but not telling you would have still changed everything whether you were in on it or not. My thoughts urge to be spoken, secrets feel like hiding, lying. I only know how to exist translucently. If I had chosen otherwise, I would have lost something of my freedom.

But

telling you was the beginning of

an odyssey.

You say so many wrong things.

Worse are all the things you leave unsaid.

Initially when I asked where we stood, you said, *We are on a friendship train*. You thought this would be reassuring, but I take metaphors seriously. This train was a limbo of ambiguity. Where was this train going? Would you detrain? What was our destination and estimated arrival time? We were a thing in motion, but blind to where we were headed and if it would justify the ride. Wanting to be the conductor, I struggled to love the train's journey as much as the two of us on it.

With time, it was clear that whatever train we were on, it couldn't be called friendship. This love became an aberration between us. Once aware of it, you were no longer friend-you. You began coddling, concealing, mixed messages spewing from your convoluted processing. It complicated my conception of how we could move forward. I begged you to behave like a normal friend. You said, *We will NEVER be normal friends*. I was devastated by this edict. You rescinded the NEVER, but it introduced fault lines in the usually uninspected label of *friend*.

We are an experiment. Who is here to ask what to do when there is no one here who knows? No one else is me and no one else is you. Who has lived as long as we in this state? Past this state to the next? We outlast the ghost stories of those who've come before. Maybe there are some that have lasted longer, but I don't know of them.

I try to level my affection with yours, but when I give less and don't love you all the way, it feels like I am not loving you at all.

I wonder what it feels like to be loved by me.
Does it hurt?
Or does it feel like a superpower?

How does the feeling differ between being loved and loving? What about when they happen synchronously in equal measure? Is that even possible? Maybe just for a millimoment?

Would it be like lightning, strikingly here then vacuously

gone?

Would it feel like a SHOUT? or a whisper?

Would it feel like I feel now? Is this *it*? Or is it something *else*? Is this enough? Can there always be more?

One of the most common "What is . . ." questions searched on Google is "What is love?" How did I understand love before I loved you? How do I understand it now? You are what society would call my *first love*. With this love being of an unrequited sort, there is a certain distance between myself and the beloved. We were not swept and falling together. I couldn't always feed the love back into you. At times, I had to hold it like a wounded bird who'd just mistaken a window for the sky. I had to watch its labored breaths and ask: What sense is there in this? Will it live or die and do I decide?

I spent this year studying love: probing friends; reevaluating the cultural references that shaped me; reading the thoughts of scientists, artists, theologians, psychologists; meditating on my history and relationship to its various forms—dissecting time with you.

I read theories on categories of love. Ancient Greek philosophers identified eight types. There is the universal love of *agape* and the self-love of *philautia*. *Ludus* is playful. *Philia* is principally a friendship love. *Eros* is romantic, sexual. *Mania* is obsessive. *Pragma* is practical and *storge* is familial. One by one I attempted to slot my love into these predefined types, searching for which could come to best define us.

agape

: a boundless altruism toward all humans, nature, and/or the divine

I learned how to spell *love* early in life. Each year when my grandmother came to visit, she would unload bags of hand-me-down clothes from her friends' older grandchildren. Somehow, a few exact-same-styled adult-sized "LOVE" T-shirts were always in the mix. Over a decade, on any given day, one of my three sisters or I could be found draped in "LOVE." No matter how big I grew, the "LOVE" would always be bigger.

Love was equivalent to *agape* in the Catholic schools I attended from kindergarten through grade twelve. It was altruistically taught as a universal ideal—a Christian channeling of the sacrificial love by capital-G God in our interactions with lowercase-*n* neighbors. *Love thy neighbor as thyself. Love is merciful. Love is charitable. Love is respect and compassion. Treat others as you would want to be treated. Even when they falter, turn the other cheek. Pay love forward.* It sounds holier-than-thou, but as a child I believed these were the rules governing society. I believe/d love is/was the base state of coexistence on a planet of human equals.

My parents enforced the application of these rules. With three sisters, fights were constant. In any interpersonal conflict at home or school, they refused to demonize my antagonist. They would ask me to consider how I might have exacerbated the situation, how I might have improved my response, how I might reformulate my interpretation of the other's intentions or sensitivities based on their possible life circumstances and insecurities to become more sympathetic. As impartial mediators equally vested in their daughters' maturations and struggles, my parents were instilling a legal system that could protect group order. If one of us was guilty, we were all guilty. In a shared space, there was no division between my experiences and feelings and those of the group. Eighteen years of this thought exercise inside a home strengthened a muscle that has become a near-instantaneous reaction to emotionally tense situations. The validity of the other is always a given and imposes upon my own. I have no choice but to find a way to love and respect the opposing perspective.

A feature of fictional Martian relationships after close observation of another is **grok**, defined as an intuitive understanding of hundreds of words "which we [humans] think of as antithetical concepts . . . [because when you understand something] so thoroughly that you merge with it and it merges with you—then you can hate it. By hating yourself. But this implies that you love it, too, and cherish it and would have it otherwise . . . 'Grok' means 'identically equal.'" As children we are taught that the opposite of love is hate, but I think they share an emotional summit, where extremes collide and all that is left to do is bow down to everyone and everything beneath.

—

Falling in love with the world didn't come until adolescence. When each daughter turned fourteen, my father took us on a father-daughter trip (daughters would pay the airfare, and help plan). I chose Venice. We left the airport in Ottawa after dinnertime. I had flown once before, that I could remember, two years prior, for the only family vacation of my childhood, to Disney World. This time, the flight was a red-eye to London. Morning came sooner than sleep. We got a connecting flight to Venice and then a boat disembarking at Piazza San Marco. By then it was somehow dinnertime again, only for me yesterday had not ended, but I was no longer the same. Standing in the piazza as pigeons flapped up and around me, that was it.

The crushing sense I suddenly had and took back with me was how much possible love lived beyond my small suburban life. Knowing it was out there but wasn't mine to inhabit felt like an injustice. I taped the tattered map of Venice above my bed. Each night standing on my mattress and following the blue pen lines crosshatching my favorite discoveries, visions were stitched back together of the tiny alleys and bridges running

over canals in Campo di Ghetto Nuovo, onward to the fish head's edge. When I closed my eyes, I could still feel the breeze coming off the lagoon. Touching the page and retelling myself its story developed a realer desire than when I had been standing inside of it. These ambulatory visions chaperoned me into dreams that I hoped would one day be reality.

Pigeons have internal compasses that allow them to find their way back to where they began, at times navigating hundreds or thousands of miles. This could be because of their heightened sense of infrasound (sounds so quiet), magnetoreception (Earth's magnetic pull), olfaction (smelling winds), and the positions of the sun and stars.

I have loved many faraways since Venice, but that trip remains my first love of somewhere else, of the hunger for the unknown and the flights that bridge them. First potent experiences are vessels to the next ones. They lay the pathways over which other similar voyages can glide onward and extend farther.

Reviewing research on grief, Maria Popova explains that through the brain's posterior cingulate cortex (a "built-in GPS of love"), we constantly process the environment and sensory information of "our loved ones' position in three dimensions—time, space, and closeness, also known as psychological distance . . . tightening the bond the closer we feel and loosening it when we sense distancing" to build a relational world map. "Within the brain, every person we love leaves a tangible, structural imprint, encoded in synapses that can never be vanquished or replaced by new and different loves." Once we know this love, it increases our ability to love others, but not in a way that replaces another love imprint.

I have a friend who theorizes each person has one thing they wake and seek from the day as a way of moving closer to love. She says for her, it's *comfort*, and for me it's *wonder*. Wonder is my gateway to love, breaching the ordinary with its specialness and educing my desire to experience it. I move closer, soaking in the essence until it becomes a part of me, and, once there, it can be used to create something I release back into the ether. Through this cycle of consumption then creation, the love roars through me.

At this age, my purpose seemed to be creator of wonder for myself and others through concocting tableaux vivants and love potions to pass around and swig. My vision sometimes fueled operatic handmade gifts, surprise events, and gestures, all for the sake of plucking at magic. I did not understand this impulse or how atypical its intensity until years later. My sister once accused me of overromanticizing things, to which I responded, "No, I think I curate my activities and environment so my exterior aligns with my interior life." Just as some people, like you, favor recollecting funny and clever anecdotes, I recollect moments of beauty and heart, dwelling in charm and earnestness. I stare into the twinkling aspects of an experience and dim the drab. When a film is veering into the sentimental, I encourage a tear. When a person shows signs of originality, I choose to be dazzled. I am a moth slapping against the porch light. I am sketching pareidolia in a cloudy life. To wear rose-colored glasses means to see things better than they are, but who decides what things actually are?

A friend leaves me a long voice message about her insecurities over feeling more intensely for her partner than he is capable of feeling toward her. Fumbling for a defense: "Feeling things is the best thing I feel." I know what she means.

In the play *The Invention of Love*, a character remarks, "Before Plato could describe love, the loved one had to be invented. We would never love anybody if we could see past our invention."

I can take for granted the tunnel of love I possess, which connects deep feeling with artmaking. I can zoom into pixels on a screen like approaching stars in a spaceship until they get larger than me and time moves fast but I feel still. I am an astronaut swimming in a gaseous atmosphere, no, I am boring to the stellar core, alone, but I don't feel alone because the hole I have made upon entry is only the size of me, snug, like I am the earplug and I cannot hear the outer sounds.

Life is my masterpiece through all the ways I choose to exert myself, visually, physically, lexiconically. In my twenties, creativity became my conduit for that wondrous love swirling the galaxy—the explicit theme of my art as I entered this phase of excess, starved and voracious for the adult world following childhood's tiny radius. My creations were messy layers of heart with ideas slamming together and invading each other, an algae bloom obstructing the white beneath from ever again reaching light. I made a canvas reading "What do you love?" coated with splatters of paint, fuzzy photocopied maps of cities I'd walked, and torn typed-out lists of my favorite films, TV shows, people, songs, and quotes, topped off with Sharpied scrawls.

Four years later, I became more inclusive, populating a sketchbook mindmap with everything I loved in every category I could conceive. I wrote teeny to leave room for more, some with question marks hanging off their ends to represent things I had yet to try but felt drawn toward. Writting in ink rather than pencil, I was conveying a confident perma- nence, or making a brazen statement against erasing my chronicle of loves.

The sketchbook listed specific things, but they didn't coincide with dis- tinctive feelings. "Love" might have been a misnomer for really liking something, though then I couldn't have known the difference. Now I see some of those things as an overstretch that reflected a **photophilic** darting toward sparks of like. Maybe I was more in love with the idea of loving specific things than loving them in actuality, or maybe I was brim- ming with the love of newness, of adult freedom to roam the earth and slurp everything all at the same time—aspirational predictions of what I would come to love. In the attempt to write what I loved, I was trying to break down my self-love—my particularities, the love particles of me.

photophilic: describes a living thing that seeks out and thrives in light

TASTES
NUTELLA ROOT BEER STREET CORN FONDANT FRENCH FRIES EDAMAME LENTILS PESTO MILK FUDGE SWEET POTATO SPRINKLES THAI FRUIT JUICE HUMMUS FRIED BREADS BRUSCHETTA TOMATO PASTE ALMOND/MARZIPAN

WORDS
DARE WONDER SCHMENGER UNKNOWING ZELIG AUDACITY SUPERNOVA ANOMALY BRIO WANDERLUST DREAM ECCENTRIC INFINITE EUDAIMONIA OTESHA SERENDIPITY

SOUNDS
ACOUSTIC COVERS NAME COMBINATIONS PIANO INSTRUMENTALS AUTOHARP SEA GULLS GYMNASTIC APPARATUS BASKETBALL SWISH RAIN OUTSIDE "I WON'T BACK S/A "BREATHE ME" DOWN

SIGHTS
MOVIE TRAILERS SMILES CARTWHEELS BUBBLES BLOWING HORIZONS MERRY-GO-ROUNDS AWARD SPEECHES CHILDREN'S ART CLASS OLD THINGS EMBROIDERY

COLOURS
INDIGO MUSTARD NAVY WHITE MINT FOREST GREEN

PLACES
FLEA MARKETS LIBRARIES VENICE mom's ARMS COASTLINES MY BED ATTICS THRIFT STORES ROOFTOPS ZANZIBAR INDIA KATHMANDU VALLEY DINERS CHINATOWNS HAMMOCK VICTORIA'S POTLUCKS

SMELLS
CHERRY SOAP VANILLA EXTRACT FRESH BAKED BREAD SALTY WATER BABIES ORANGE MAPLE FREESIE GASOLINE CREASES OF OLD CUT GRASS BOOKS

NATURE
OCEAN RAINY DAYS PEACOCK BREEZES BLOWN DANDELIONS FLOCKS OF BIRDS SNOW BEFORE CHERRY BLOSSOM FALLING CHRISTMAS WILLOWS SWAY ROLLING HILLS BANYAN CLING CONSTELLATIONS FROM SOUTHERN HEMISPHERE AUTUMN LEAVES SUNFLOWERS - FIELDS NEPALI MONKEYS YELLOW

GARDEN?
TON
GING
CLIMBING
YOGA CANOE
HULA HOOP
UNTEERING
CLING
ES
EATING
ING
TRIPS
ANGUAGE

?

The capacity to inhabit love has matured with me, but my criteria for designating something as "love" has contracted and become more abstract.

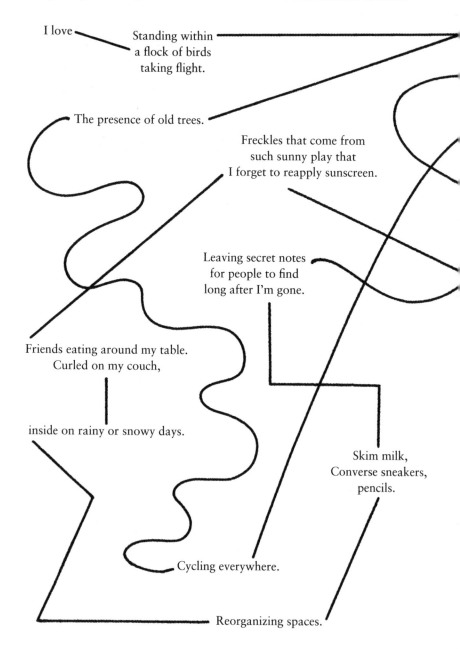

I love

Standing within
a flock of birds
taking flight.

The presence of old trees.

Freckles that come from
such sunny play that
I forget to reapply sunscreen.

Leaving secret notes
for people to find
long after I'm gone.

Friends eating around my table.
Curled on my couch,

inside on rainy or snowy days.

Skim milk,
Converse sneakers,
pencils.

Cycling everywhere.

Reorganizing spaces.

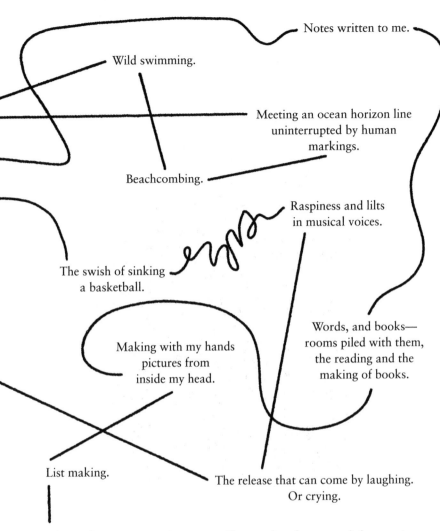

Notes written to me.

Wild swimming.

Meeting an ocean horizon line
uninterrupted by human
markings.

Beachcombing.

Raspiness and lilts
in musical voices.

The swish of sinking
a basketball.

Making with my hands
pictures from
inside my head.

Words, and books—
rooms piled with them,
the reading and the
making of books.

List making.

The release that can come by laughing.
Or crying.

I love when someone gives me a gift or orders for me and they get it right: they get me. I love trying new things and being startled when I love them; I love that there are things that still exist that I haven't tried, untapped sources of love available.

On my own, this list of love has slowed and settled, mostly only growing now through others, through experiencing loved ones' love of things that I would never have come to love on my own, that I love more because they are entwined with a person I love.

I send you a postcard while on vacation in Mexico.

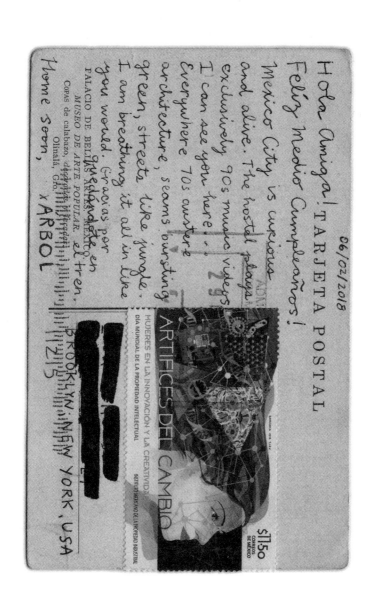

06/02/2018

Hola Amiga! TARJETA POSTAL
Feliz Medio Cumpleaños!
Mexico City is curious
and alive. The hostel plays
exclusively 90s music videos
I can see you here.
Everywhere 70s austere
architecture, seams bursting
green, streets like jungle.
I am breathing it all in like
you would. Gracias por
quererme tanto.
Home soon,
x ARBOL

BROOKLYN, NEW YORK, USA

ARTIFICES DEL CAMBIO

MUJERES EN LA INNOVACIÓN Y LA CREATIVIDAD
DÍA MUNDIAL DE LA PROPIEDAD INTELECTUAL
INSTITUTO MEXICANO DE LA PROPIEDAD INDUSTRIAL

$11.50
CORREOS
DE MÉXICO

Copas de calabaza, detalle
PALACIO DE ARTE POPULAR
MUSEO DE BELLAS ARTES
MUSEO DE ARTE POPULAR, el tren.
Olinalá, Gto.

I photograph all the different plants to show you.

I travel differently now . . . maybe because I am emulating the way you travel: slowly, socially, locally . . . I loiter in reverence more, don't move as fast past a scene, follow my friends' leads. I don't think I would have reveled in the geobotany of Mexico without your influence. You brought nature inside. I became a homeowner of houseplants. A mother to mine and an aunt to yours. You knew I would be their stand-in provider when you went away. All of them, too many to count, encircling every window and surface that rays might reach. Jars of propagated cuttings, mugs of seedlings, pots of trees, climbing vines, and hanging planters.

You keep a Sunday ritual. A podcast playing, large plants migrate to the bathtub for their shower, mounds of soil pile around the dining room during repotting, the kitchen sink a clinic for treating disease. Empathy for the natural was a growing part of how I felt connected to the world, but I had never observed how this care could be adopted in the home. Fully occupied, you socialize with the plants like they're a lively occasion. I watched you watch them. I watched too. crouching down. tilting my head. scrunching my eyes in close. To cheer for the first prick of a sprout, grimace at a crinkled leaf, observe greens creeping to yellows or surging verdantly. I love how you always buy the nearly dead, depressed plants—the prospect of their survival and unforeseen transformation astonishes. Maybe being wanted would will them stalwart. We watched those that grew and those that died with equal tenderness.

I remember the day you showed me the community garden near our house, with the willow and pagoda and managed wildness. I keeled over with an identical strike of torrential love that suffused my insides as in the flash when I fell for you—
vertiginous,
blood pumping loud,
guts in quicksand,
diverted airflow,
legs so weak.

IN ANCIENT GREECE, THE COLOR TO DESCRIBE THE GREEN OF PLANTS WAS THE SAME AS FOR THE COLOR OF HUMAN SKIN.

I longed to join a community garden,
and you brought it forth.

You gave me green.

Now I see all plants. The ones poking out of sidewalk cracks, the ugly
and pretty, the ways they change from place to place, the ways they are
alike and ever so tacitly unlike.

I love that even though you think it's silly that I anthropomorphize my
plants, you remember each of their names. I love how when we go plant
shopping you will let me pick our new plantmates.

I love how a vase of flowers will unexpectedly appear in my bedroom.
You know sunflowers are my favorite because they interminably follow
the light.

I know yours are heliconia, their nectar attracting **hummingbirds**.

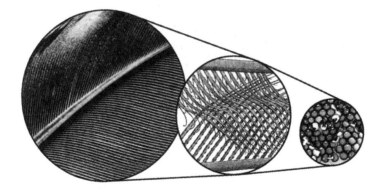

broad-billed hummingbird: Blue is the rarest pigment in nature. In almost all
cases, what we perceive as blue is a trick of the eye. Hummingbird feathers have a
prismatic nanostructure of layered air bubbles that refract light off a mosaic of inner
and outer angled surfaces to optically simulate an iridescent blue-green shimmer in
the viewer's eyes.

I once made this self-portrait

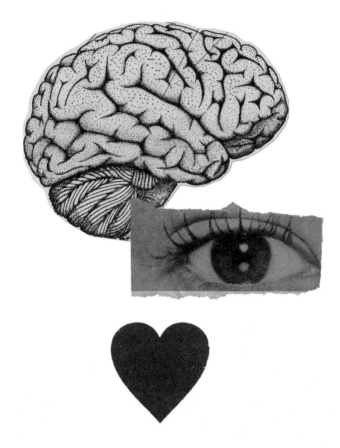

I often have difficulty delineating a love for the universe from a love of self. I am drawn to the world through wonder, and it enters and exists in me through making, so it is hard to say where one ends and the other begins. What would be left to love in oneself if not echolocating off of the world?

I see a DIY video of an artist demonstrating the ancient Japanese marbling technique of *Suminagashi* ("ink floating"). He places an empty wooden picture frame in rainwater gathered in brooks, the hollows of rock surfaces, puddles. He takes one paintbrush and dips it in a cup of soapy water, takes another paintbrush and dips it in Indian ink, and then he delicately drums the brush tips in the water held by the frame as the two introduced liquids mix and ripple outward in psychedelic blob patterns. Finally, paper is laid atop the swirls in the frame and then lifted to capture the print. When I see this technique of hiking into a forest and squatting over pools of water to make experimental art, all I can think is that if I were not to do this alone, you are the only person I would ever want to bring along, I know you would need no convincing. There is usually a divine aloneness required for me to experience wonder, but when you are near, rather than that wonder quieting, it echoes. In harmonic relations, sympathetic resonance is created when a body begins to vibrate in response to a vibratory body brought close to it. I knew that morning when we crawled into a thicket and picked wild black, red, and white berries that the delirious ringing in my ears from the discovery was a ringing you could hear too.

I huddled in close as liquid globules were added one by one to the glass in third-grade science class. *See how the liquid curves above the lip?* my teacher boasted. *That's called the* **meniscus**. *We must go slow so the edges hold.* A convex meniscus is observed when the liquid's particles are more attracted to each other than to their container. A concave meniscus occurs when the particles are more drawn to their container than to themselves. Does the meniscus spill over when it becomes attracted not to itself or its container but to that which lies beyond? I think more likely most of the time I am a meniscus held together by my insides and the outsides acting equally upon one another, only an eggshell-thin divider between.

Our mail slot spills letters from charitable organizations. I love how you sign all the street-fundraising petitions for causes requesting support then promptly turn stone-cold once they mail-stalk you.

What might feel selfless seems rooted in selfishness, of using acts of altruism to inflate one's self-worth and prove one's goodness against the creeping guilt inherited from a judging society. This doesn't diminish the act, but it does nod to a codependency between love of self and love of everything else.

My parents were overstretched. The way I best proved my love to them was through minimizing household burdens: asking for little and offering a lot of physical and emotional support. It was my earliest form of making: making the house ordered was how I could demonstrate love and, in gratitude, how my parents could offer it back. My drive to "do good" comes from this wanting to earn my status in relationships and community, to be valuable so as not to be discarded or disconnected. I will spend all day lugging awkward objects to assist with a friend's move; bring them a care package and a consoling shoulder when they are distraught; perspicaciously work through their blocks in a professional or personal project; and say yes to any request of any sort from anyone asking for help. If enough people appreciate me, my inner voice must follow suit. Maybe this drive emerged from my upbringing. Maybe it is preternatural.

By contrast, your altruism seems more purely spawned from struggles in your childhood. Those developmental hurdles and traumatic events that exposed you too early and cruelly to a feeling of powerlessness. Maybe when you hear someone's tragic circumstances, read a news article about injustice, or learn of a friend or client's staggering predicament, it hearkens back to that helpless enclosure. You empathize, donate, offer services, and then briefly, in your personal world, go limp in order to recover. I think you permit yourself to feel more through another's suffering than you do from your own pains, long ago erecting safeguards against your unnavigable vulnerabilities.

Through altruism I redeem a feeling of belonging to others.
Through altruism you redeem a feeling of belonging to yourself.

philautia

: a self-love

I began fiercely independent, my mother says. Too engrossed in personal fascinations and individuation to bother calculating my quality vis-à-vis peers. I also seemed to be perennially preparing for future singledom. The message of self-reliance was there, but I was more attuned to it than a typical five-eight-eleven-teen-year-old. As the oldest of four I was left alone a lot, left in charge, a third parent. Women in our family only know to walk through fires on their own, my mother says.

I was meticulous and hardworking by nature: homework done promptly, bedroom straightened daily, art projects self-initiated in my off-hours. I was most drawn to activities that I could own: stockpiling treasures found in gutters, hand-making a monthly house newspaper, cutting and pasting images and letters out of magazines, drawing and decorating floor plans and maps of fictional places, and crafting characters and worlds inside my head. It felt like my entire childhood was lived inside my head.

This nature might explain why my unrequited love flourished. I am comfortable loving with some distance, my inner landscape a reliable location for threshing a feeling from its stalk to admire in isolation. In my possession, unadulterated from outside breaches, creative forces have a multiplier effect on the original feeling.

Even through adolescence, I retained a love for the unique self that I'd procured, which felt distancing from the theatrics observed in the teen experience around me. In middle school, my vice principal sang Black Eyed Peas' "Where Is the Love?" a cappella at the beginning of school assemblies (all of which felt themed around anti-bullying, anti-smoking campaigns). Two hundred thirteen-year-olds fidgeted in awkwardness on the shellacked wooden gymnasium floor, averting the vice principal's impassioned stare. It was that merciless age when everyone was so confused by hormones, crushing rejections, and boyfriends stolen that their self-acceptance was held in another's gaze. I felt none of it. With each stanza, there was a desperation in her voice. I wanted to know where their love went as well.

I have always been told my *philautia* is abnormal. But I am told a lot of me is abnormal. Acquaintances tag me an original, an oddity, a some-thing else, not broken or unlovable, just scarcely mirrored. I feel it too. Admired more than understood. Though now that I am old enough to have bonded with many people, I reckon my core is no weirder than anyone else's, it simply has an aversion to conformity, more comfortable flexing than masking itself.

I attempt to find studies about people who just *have* self-love from the start. There are none that I can locate. Self-love is framed as an aspiration not an attestation. I ask my sister:

ME: Why do you think I have always had self-love?
SISTER: I don't know. What do you mean?
ME: Like, not wanting to be someone else, accepting my
           ways as worthwhile.
SISTER: Wait, I have that too. Are we not supposed to have it?
ME: That is what I am trying to figure out. What was it
           about Mom and Dad and the way we were brought
           up that made us so centered?
SISTER: I don't know, maybe because Mom and Dad are that
           way too, inward. But not, like, in a way that seems
           self-obsessed . . .
ME: True, they are kind of selfish in their devotions, but it
           feels more existential than egotistical.

I can want things that others have, but I never want to be them or to swap out my traits for theirs. Self-improvement is a rivalry between who I was and who I will be, and who I am in the interim is plenty. I embrace the stuff that makes me. I believe I am so very possible, anthemic, clever without subtracting kindness, a spinner of criticism into revelation. An expert list-maker and box-checker. I come to each day like a blank canvas, trusting the strokes necessary to complete the big picture. I am not afraid of where my mind goes when felled or how it will grow back up wiser.

If I wasn't this actualized, we couldn't have endured your rejection.

Though, one gaping hole in my self-love permanently aggravates my rejected state.

—

Before I tell you I love you, I have to explain my sexuality. It is not a secret so much as not a solid shape. I am not in or out, I am just me. And in the seldom instances where I feel a simmering physical attraction to another, it is always a combination of things, and never exclusively or dominantly sexual in form. There is no trauma or repression or a fear of intimacy in my past. This is how I have always felt in relation to other bodies, only aware of its oddness through society's portrayals of "healthy" and "normal." Here I write no resolute delineations of what my sexual predilections are or are not. I cannot know how I will feel in the future or how I will feel with every person.

There are labels, so many labels that I have sought to apply . . . *bisexual, sapiosexual, asexual, biromantic demisexual, queer* . . . there are not enough labels to encapsulate the qualities that might attract me to another person. This attraction seldom manifests wholly and robustly in one person. I might be attracted to a person's voice, or insight, or atmosphere, and it can be completely independent of what I think of their physical appearance or level of overall compatibility with me as a partner. They are puny tingles of attraction that come with the greatest infrequency. So, we've not spoken of my sexuality before because there is little certainty that can be exposed, and I have left unuttered an identity that exists insofar as it is not contained.

When I began probing my own sexuality on the spectrum, back before fluidity became a cultural trend, I saw this talk show clip of an asexuality spokesperson trying to explain the isolation that is felt by an asexual in a society that inextricably binds sex with love, intimacy, happiness, and sense of self, asserting the supremacy of sex above all other experiences and interactions. The interviewer was quick to dismiss him as probably being repressed, confused as to why it was even a topic worth discussing, as if lacking the need for sex meant he also lacked the need for love.

Angela Chen writes: "To explain asexuality and what it means to not experience sexual attraction, aces must define and describe the exact phenomena we don't experience. It requires us to use the language of 'lack,' claiming we are legitimate in spite of being deficient, while struggling to explain exactly what it is we don't get."

It wasn't until my mid-twenties, after enough misencounters in dating to feel certain of my "lack," that a double mourning overcame me as I began to understand how absent sexual attraction was from my personhood. In Mandarin, there are 113 terms for *shame*. I inherited two: *xiu chi* and *xiu kui*. **Xiu chi** is a feeling of social failure and threat to one's public identity. Based on the dominant discourse about sex, I feel ashamed of my predisposition to antisexualism and my limited sexual experiences. Like I am considered stunted and begin to believe it too. **Xiu kui** is a feeling of personal failure and threat to one's private identity. In comparing myself to the testimonies of women around me, I worried that I was anatomically incapable of knowing *love*-love. At first, I briefly hated myself, like I had been hung upside down and slaughtered halal-style. Then it turned more into hating my circumstance, faith in a happy ending stolen from me by an exclusionary society.

I can see how in my New York bubble gender roles and relationship structures are slowly being unboxed, but the last two decades of life have felt like being moved from one makeshift waiting room to another, waiting to finally be invited into a space where I make sense.

Sometimes I wonder how much of my time is spent trying to maintain exceptionalism so as to compensate for not appearing pitiful in singleness. Perfection is a prerequisite for nothing, but there is so much time in singleness to try. And unfortunately, there is something exceptional about you, or how I respond to you, whether because of my sexuality or all of me, that has manifested a certain kind of love in me that has not yet been able to redirect toward a new beloved whose acceptance might override your rejection, so I am left laboring over the qualities that earn me self-acceptance.

I am chock-full of love. I have made beautiful friendships, creations, and experiences across the globe. So many adventures and passions that steady me. I try to appreciate that, without sexual distraction and satisfaction, I spent my twenties cultivating other forms of love. Now knowing what love feels like—when a person gets inside you and you can't feel around yourself for a while, when you start questioning your decisions, when you want to be fused with another person and that togetherness feels like everything—I can't imagine what I would have become if that had happened to me from the time of teen crushes into adulthood, when there were so many choices to be made, so much inner voice required to gulp the world. Instead of that kind of all-consuming love, I prioritized goals that were within my control. Me the **mudlark** plucking phrases and ideas and new sensations of the self out of changing environs. I hope, though can never know, that my sexual orientation has given as much as it's taken.

In response to my pains with unrequited love, a friend asks me, *If you love yourself, what's the problem?*

Erik Erikson's popular theory of psychosocial development tracks the stages of an individual's growth from childhood through adulthood. To successfully move through "Stage 5: Identity versus Confusion" during adolescence, one explores *Who am I?* and *What do I want?*, emerging with a strong sense of self, independence, and agency. I did that. Next

mudlark: someone who grubs in muddy shore for valuable objects

comes "Stage 6: Intimacy versus Isolation," which spans two decades. The central question during this time is *Can I love and be loved?*, seeking long-lasting, supportive relationships.

Self-love is enough until it isn't.

My friend told me of a therapy session wherein she talked about being afraid of becoming dependent on a partner, knowing that she had to be okay by herself. Her therapist responded, *Why? Why is it a bad thing to depend on others? That makes you human. We need people and that's okay.* Whoa. I was raised to not need a man, not get trapped out of need, not to lose myself in the preoccupying and pleasing of another, not be weakened through being supported. But I took self-sufficiency to the extreme. I mastered the art of thriving in aloneness. Then I met you. Now, I want people, a want that is actually a need. I had people before, but not intimately, familially, codependently in the way that I now crave. You made me want to entangle myself in the lives of others.

—

A decade ago, my art projects were preoccupied with that which distinguished me, listing everything that I loved like no one else. I looked inward. Inadvertently, nearly ten years later, I begin an art project that aims to uncover all the things that everyone else in my life loves. I look outward. In the lead-up to my thirtieth year, I make a recommendations form to expand my influences through the obsessions of others. I send forms to a hundred people. I ask artists, writers, old teachers, bosses, travel companions, exes, friends, and family—those I met long ago and those I see every day. People who have walked through my life leaving traces. People who are still on the edges of entry. I ask them to fill out a form that I will gather and bind into a book to inspire my next decade.

Name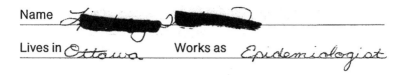

Lives in *Ottawa*   Works as *Epidemiologist*

Recommendations!

Book *The 13 Clocks - James Thurber*

Film *Coraline*

TV Show *Brooklyn 99*

Song *Jazzman - Carole King*

Person *Stephanie Nolen*

Place *Monteverde, Costa Rica*

Thing *Sunflowers (also easy to grow!)*

Food *Sunshine Lentil Bowls*

Activity *Cycling*

Word *Transcendent*

Quote/Concept *"To me, you shall be unique in all the world" - The Little Prince*
"Of course it is happening inside your head, but why on earth should that mean that it is not real?" - Albus Dumbledore

Other *"One loves the sunset when one is so sad" - The Little Prince.*
Have a beautiful year, my love.

Name C███████ ███

Lives in BROOKLYN   Works as TELEPHONE OPERATOR

Recommendations!

Book PHANTOM PAINS OF MADNESS - NOELLE KOCOT

Film GIRLFRIENDS - CLAUDIA WEILL

TV Show FRIDAY NIGHT LIGHTS (SEASON 1)

Song SWEEDEEDEE - MICHAEL HURLEY

Person CLARA PORSET - CHAIR MAKER

Place TEN THOUSAND WAVES IN SANTA FEW
(GO AT NIGHT IN WINTER)

Thing A BLUE METAL CHAIR, A CASIO
KEYBOARD

Food CUBAN MASHED POTATOES FROM PILAR

Activity LAYING BACKWARD ON YOUR BED

Word FLORID / HONEYED

Quote/Concept

THE HEART HOARDS ITS THORNS
JUST AS THE ROSE PROFLIGATES.
JUST BECAUSE YOU'VE HAD ENOUGH
DOESN'T MEAN YOU WANTED TOO MUCH.
- DEAN YOUNG

Other THE SMELL OF CEDAR / BRUSHING
YOUR HAIR INTO A CURTAIN IN FRONT
OF YOUR FACE / LISTENING TO CHOPIN

Recommendations!

eyes: ambar lucid — even if its a lie: matt maltese
hourglass: catfish and the bottlemen
we're going to be friends: the white stripes
you and me: penny and the quarters

pretty girl: clairo
5.05: Abba

Name A▮▮▮▮▮▮
generation why: conan grey
pulling leaves please: off trees :(

yeah right: joji
♡ ♡♡ happy 29th bday! ily! canada!
Grade 10 Merivale high school
wallows

SLOW DANCING IN THE DARK: joji
bellyache
multi-love: unkown mortal orchestra
Palace tomal, Make me your queen, why do you feel so down: Declan McKenna
in your neighbours garden: mimi mimi

come out and play: billie eilish
buttercup: jack stauber
blondie: current joys
Walking all day: graham coxon

hostage
Kevin's heard: J. Cole

I won't hurt you: The west coast pop art experimental band

Book   the perks of being a wall flower
Bobby: beaba-doobee

and

Film   extremely loud, incredibly close, Pulp Fiction, Isle of dogs

TV Show   The Office, End of the Fxxxing World
spead dial: beadadoobee

You're the first, the last, my everything: Barry white

Song   The night we met, Love like ghosts : lord huron
B-A-B-Y: Carla Thomas   Maybe: RICEWINE
All I want: Kodaline

and

Person   joji (hes a cool guy, but he has really good music)
American boy: Estelle

we might be dead tomorrow -Soko

Place   ☆ City of Nice, France

Thing   thrift stored clothes, dollarama stickers, coffee with lots of sugar ♡
or ramen

Food   miso soup with shrimp tempura, dumplings and rice noodles with beef onions and bean sprouts

milkshakes from Zac's diner

Activity   stargazing

pumped up kicks: foster the people

Word   Anhedonia, alexithymia, eunoia, psithurism, balter

billy joel: piano man

木漏れ日 (komorebi)
Quote/Concept

Strange magic : electric light orchestra

the days we stay up late to not forget the secrets
the sun told that day, the bittersweet taste of what used
to be, but the world rests behind your eyelids as you
fall into slumber, days passing by too fast right now,
turning into memories of the past, a month in a week

four leaf clover: christain hudson

you never can tell: chuck berry

Other   i have so many good songs to give you and i wote
really messily and tiny but i hope you get all of them.
some of them are a bit weird. Sorri. i didn't get a chance to

put your records on: corinne Bailey Rae
build me up buttercup
starman: David Bowie
write all of them if you want
write all of them, i have LOADS MORE!
you can't hurry love: the supremes

Name M████████

Lives in _Your Home_   Works as ~~████████████████~~.

Recommendations!

Book ~~████████████████████████████~~

Film ~~You already know them all...~~ ~~████████████~~

TV Show ~~████████████████████████████~~

Song ~~████████████████████████████~~

Person ~~████████████████████~~ ♡

Place ~~████████████████████████████~~

Thing ~~████████████████████████████~~

Food ~~████████████████████████████~~

Activity ~~████████████████████████████~~

Word ~~████████████~~

Quote/Concept ~~████████████████████████████~~
~~████████████████████████████~~
~~████████████████████████████~~
~~████████████████████████████~~
~~████████████████████████████~~
~~████████████████████████████~~

Other ~~████████████████████████████~~

I used to be about claiming the peculiars. The less I was like others, the more I was of me, immaculately conceived. An unsullied clarity of mind and world view only mine. But while some of my loves are tried and true, others get expended and usurped. And life is long, there is time and room to be contaminated and still retain **haecceity**.

You brought me to a point where the experience of loving another human and watching the ways they experience love, in the deepest and completest sense, is the most desired and least ventured love in my life. I am ready for my thisness to include *us*ness and *you*ness and *else*ness.

—

haecceity: "thisness"; the particular essence of a thing, the qualities that set it apart

I tell you of Canadian memories—French loanwords, Sarah McLachlan's "Ice Cream," Hula-Hoop records, fairy friends, snow days, and yearnings for uniforms and sidewalks and attics. I tell you about how in first grade I filled up on Valentine's sweets as I was getting the stomach flu and spent the evening vomiting pink froth pocked with candy hearts reading

We watch clips of Canadian and European-imported shows of my youth. When my days are not so smiley, you send me heartening stills from the Swiss Claymation series *Pingu*, because no matter how gloomy my day, a malleable kid-**penguin** crafting with glitter always brings happy.

penguin: Many penguin species collect rocks to elevate their nests so the eggs won't drown during rain or snowmelt. A male penguin will scour for the ideal pebble to offer as a gift to the female penguin he wishes to court. The female will add the pebble to her nest if she accepts.

Your childhood sounded happy. So much time in nature, parents and friends that let you be you. I did not know but would have loved child-you. The you that wore different colored overalls almost every day because you *didn't like feeling fabrics*. The you that wanted to be Jane Goodall, memorized baseball stats, baked loaves of cranberry bread for charity, amassed hotel soaps, had a tape recorder to recount your dreams, kept a real cat called Boots and a stuffed cat called Window.

I wonder what it would have been like for child-me to have a friend like child-you. I would have told you that one day, our lives would blaze brighter than we could ever have imagined. I would have told you not to let your speech **block** stymie your spunk as it did.

You mention the block casually, maybe five months into living together. We were sitting at the dining room table snacking, the other two housemates in earshot but generally disengaged, making dinner foods. Something about how you didn't outgrow it until your early twenties, that for most of your life the block made you snag in silence midway through speaking, words that wouldn't come out, how that block made you look down instead of toward the horizon, believing you would never reach it. For a time, it strangled your self-worth and kept you from knowing the thrill of possibility that your future would hold.

When I was nineteen I dated a boy with a stutter for a summer. He regularly struggled with a sentence, it was stressful, like both our airways constricting. I would relax my facial expression and try to transfer sedate thoughts to him. It never worked to smooth out the sentence, it wasn't a mental block, it was bodily, like the tongue forgot its job as the brain's microphone. I read articles about the shame that can develop in a child

block: also referred to as *dysfluent speech*, is "the disruption of the forward flow and timing of speech by repetition of sounds, syllables, or words; sound prolongation; and/or blocking on sounds, silent or audible." This is different than a pause in speech caused by a grappling with ideas to express next.

with a speech impediment in social settings. Not wanting to be "found out" and perceived as "stupid," the dysfluency creates an aversion to speaking and a general hypervigilance around others. I read about the iceberg analogy of stuttering wherein 20 percent of the experience is observable through the block itself and the other 80 percent exists as covert feelings of guilt, fear, anxiety, and avoidance. This boy was chatty, suave, snubbing to his stutter. We didn't date long enough for me discover if he had always been that way or how long it took to get there.

I am astounded by your strength, trying to grasp your experience without much firsthand accounting. I wish you would have divulged more of how you thought it wired you, the ways that you think it still impacts how you spiral and sit in space, particularly the silent spaces between us.

When I hear about your youth, it sounds like you endured that block with fortitude. That you learned to eloquently anticipate and craft phrases to avoid it. I don't remember you presenting your former block as a secret, but it felt highly classified, sensitive, not for me to prod or reintroduce into conversation unless you brought it up, which you did seldomly in cases where you still felt its ramifications, when it might briefly show up in an indiscernible pause. I only know a little of most of the defining moments in your life. Those that have the potential to paint an entire world view in chiaroscuro. You open enough to provide little incident reports—a few sentences of takeaways stated before you close back up, unlikely to reference the event again. Any other friend of mine would loop back to such experiences over the years when providing advice, as anecdote regarding my current struggle. This kind of exercise is how two people approach the belief that however different in shape their trials and tribulations may take, they amount to similar vistas.

Without the opportunity to co-explore our internal landscapes, I get stuck in endless comparing-and-contrasting cycles that begin to create a chasm in my mind between our personalities, I being of some inferior quality but also opposite of whatever you are. If you are quiet, I must be loud. You are easy and I am difficult. Gentle/brash. Considered/hasty. Empathetic/apathetic. Desirable/desirous. It obscures how similar we might actually be.

Often I feel no need to report aloud my cogitations. But with you, I feel an urgency to speak every pretty thing, to quote something moving that I have read, to describe the glory of the scene in front of us, to let you in on the magic that has arrived in your presence. "It is not the voice that commands the story: it is the ear." It's as if those thoughts force themselves to the surface because of a kinship in the room where they might aerate while retaining their sacredness in the same way that they percolate when alone. But you don't invite those thoughts into the conversation. And I don't often then speak them. But perhaps the very nature of their existence is predicated on this ambient entente.

Of course, I don't actually know what you feel when you are in this room or when alone. I don't know if this sacredness appears to you as the prize that it does to me, or if you are scouring for something else in your landscape. It must not be as totalizing for you since it doesn't amount to a love of me.

On the challenges of translation in literature, Richard Kearney wrote, "It is the right of every living tongue to speak itself and, moreover, to be translated into other tongues while retaining a certain reservoir of irreducible, untranslatable intimacy. Each dialect has its secrets." Would he have considered our shared language dyadic, or two distinct reservoirs?

I sometimes think that the biggest difference in our wiring by childhood worlds is that you learned to push feelings down, I, to push feelings out. We were a household encouraged to verbalize our feelings, leaping from feeling them to controlling them through the power of oration. Uncertainty was not an inhabited state. What if all that saying and dissecting deceived me into feeling confident in who I was and what I felt, as if saying was an absolute extension of feeling—brain to tongue?

What if the muscle strengthened wasn't that of understanding but of translating the self, and my interpretation was premature? In contrast, how did you make sense of yourself in silence?

You know you are right exactly the way you are?
Don't you?
You are everything-everything you need to be in this moment.

Okay?

I want you to trust this. I want you to love yourself more than I do.
I want you to love yourself more than I want you to love me.

ludus

: a playful, childlike connection of fun and games
without commitment

In retrospect, the earliest seedling from which my love for you might have sprung was our first venture outside the house as we moved from being housemates to friends. A trip to the Metropolitan Museum of Art. A museum can be a disjointed activity for even the closest of friends, each person's pace and degree of absorption so varied. But I was stunned after whipping through a too-crowded and underwhelming da Vinci exhibition to find you right next to me.

We wafted lackadaisically through most of the galleries until becoming enchanted by the same painting. *Lorette in a Green Robe, Black Background.* A Matisse. The caption read that this was when Matisse began "to use black as a color of light and not as a color of darkness." So much of my lifeblood is braced by this notion. You said you would hang this in your house. I would too. I said I could paint a reproduction of it. And for your birthday I did. Now it does hang in our house (that is, its substandard imitation). For the robe color, I mixed an acrylic aqua blue (pigments: PG7, PW6, PB15) with an emerald green (pigments: PG7, PW6, PY74)—the blue and the green sharing two of their three compounds, not the same but an overlapping close. We favor the greens and blues—you leaning more toward a greenish blue, me more toward a bluish green.

Sometimes I dream we are in a silent film standing in front of the original. Not touching or talking or even acknowledging the other. We are strangers or we are reuniting after years estranged, brought into Lorette's nest for a chimed hush, hammock hung. My mind freezes the film here, rewinding and replaying this scene, uncomplicated by the feelings that will follow.

When it comes to film, if we are not careful, we'll spend a whole night cascading from one trailer to the next without settling on something to watch. I used to love trailers, often more than full-length films. Why watch a two-hour unfolding when a two-minute reel doses us with its diapason? The most piercing lines. slapstick antics. cropped faces devolving

OVER 12 MONTHS, MATISSE PAINTED
LORETTE SOME 50 TIMES.

SHE WAS HIS FIRST OBSESSION OF
LOVE THAT FLOWED OUT ON CANVAS.

into anguish or ecstasy. interspersed with snippets of cinematic scapes: sparklers sizzling; crowds erupting; blurred backgrounds as heroes run fast-fast or thunder dance; aerial shots of terrestrial marvels and emphatic heavens; all strung together with an instrumental score building to plucky indie folk or triumphal pop-music release.

Why watch the whole film? Why? Because we haven't earned the trailer's dose. If there is already a danger of seeking the film version of our lives, the trailer version is even more abbreviated. We have to do the work of aliveness every minute, all the days. I swear some minutes are so monotonous that I have seen seasons change between the seconds. And then there are days, weeks, months, that have sped by with such celerity that my body can only assume catatonia to prevent disintegration upon atmospheric reentry to the present's pace. Idleness gives way to inspiration, repetition to spontaneity, a slow drip to a downpour. Moments of nothing inform moments of everything. I can't rush to the end of our story. And why would I want to? Trailers offer the highlights without the substance. The emotions are not linked to context or the development of the characters in relation to their inner selves and outer lives. Life is not about the extreme ends but the in-betweens that string us together across space and time. This year was not a trailer for love, not even a film. It was 31,536,000 seconds long. Sure, there were beams of euphoria, saccharine settings, fractional dramatics—the stuff of trailers.

But mostly,
it contained a sundry
of microscopic
    earnest,
    brave,
    and sublime
    vestiges.

And time enough to watch and make and play many things.

—

We attempt to watch trendy new docuseries and critically acclaimed films that ready us for dinner-party chatter, but we are more likely to retreat to the classics, like bad 2000s chick flicks that bring guffawing appall and good 1990s chick flicks that bring nostalgic veneration.

We watch your preferences more than mine. Maybe because you're pickier and I am thirstier for exposure to your familiar. I am envious of the refined quiddity of your taste, some of which has come from repetition. I love so many things, you so few. I am more experimental than addictive, sampling and moving on because there is too much untraveled to justify treading the old. When it comes to listening and watching and reading, you are more entertained in the re's: relistening, rewatching, rereading—you return to what you loved once and keep loving it in the revisits.

Sometimes while we watch you will suddenly climax in laughter and I will be smitten by your ability to be so quickly and fully exulted. I love the variable sounds of your laughs. The realest one is the rarest: a squeaky hyperventilation that is seldom set off by anyone other than your interwoven bestest lifelong friend. What of you I will ever know is limited by how little I know of her. She serves as a constant reminder of how epic our friendship could be if only you were at ease—you speak of her with effusive admiration; mail her gifts for no occasion; dig through city archives to construct a vivid bridesmaid speech; you radiate upon return from nature trips with her; and in your hours-long weekly phone calls, the house's frame shudders from laughter. Once when she was visiting, there was a sudden *boom!* because the two of you were laughing so hard she fell off the bed and concussed her head. I wish I could make you laugh like that. I don't know what will make you laugh, though I don't know what will make me laugh either. Sometimes I say something that sets off the second-best laugh: a drumming cackle accompanied by glossy eyes. When it comes, I freeze. I try to open my ears and alert my memory to record such a sound: the crackling symphony of a heart unlocking.

You love when someone can make you laugh, but most times you are the engineer of laughter. Finding comedy in the stories you've chosen to retell, you speak through jilted squeals like a body spurting dopamine. The sound alone is a splash of happy to my body. I love your impersonations— pitch-perfect imitations of lines from funny shows and stand-up routines delivered verbatim. They come from your appreciation of comic relief.

Without intentionally attempting humor, I make other friends laugh more often than I do you. I want you to find levity in me like you do with your closest friends. When I am not around, do you retell stories of mine you thought were funny? Do you retell stories of mine and make them funny?

—

You defy my prejudgments often. The more I learn of you, the more you surprise.

Like: how you cry watching marathons
Like: how you fancy parades, the Ball Drop,
          when families gather for barbecues in the park
Like: how committed and theatrical and cute you become
          when playing charades
Like: how you enjoy projecting the Yule Log video
          extra large on the wall at Christmas
Like: no matter how I imagine conversations
          or interactions
          or activities with you transpiring,
          they never go as anticipated.

—

We are floor people.

I think our friendship began with floor. This was before you were granted open invitation to my room whether or not I was present. Before the near-nightly rendezvous. About a week after I moved in, you came home to find me on my floor building a makeshift loom. You pranced in, probably for the first time, past the popular seating choices of desk chair, armchair, ottoman, bed, and rugs and sat next to me on the hardwood, supervising with inquisitive delight over this quirky endeavor. I was charmed by your eagerness, by the lightness with which you fast-tracked intimacy and the warmth of a cheerleader as the drill befuddled me. This might have been the first time we found ourselves at eye level rather than passings by on stairs. It was here that you assumed your preferred stretch position of legs straight, hands clasped around pointed toes, back folding deeply. My preferred position is crossed legs, head drooping into hands and collapsing onto floor.

Sometimes we would craft on floor. Eat on floor. Watch TV, sketch, open gifts, play games, online shop, fold laundry, crossword, and read, all on floor. When we feel a funk, when stress becomes us, when the world is too much, we lie on floor. It is our default plane for dithyrambic ramblings, daily recaps, and private thoughts that must be uttered but make us spin, make us laugh—cry—lurch. Floor grounds us, in ourselves, yes, but also in each other. I can feel you through the floor (both while we are together but also unnervingly when you move throughout the house, every creaky floorboarded step reminding of your distance). It didn't matter which floor. All floors our shared base. Floor frees motions, permitting contortion of body to pantomime the largesse of emotions. It is unmoving, and so are we, in staying the course. I love that floor is ours, a planet upon which no others shall visit, meant only to withstand the weight of two.

I love escaping reality into our planet.

You suggest hanging paper **cranes** for a tea party. We fold two hundred. You get really quiet and focus on the folding.

I start to jabber.

You say, *Sshhh, can't talk, I'm craning.*

I smile, bite my lip. I get happy feeling you get lost in a happy that I am part of creating for us.

We fall into the folding.

I love how paper softens in its creases. I am drawn to the worn. The more something is used, the more it appears loved.

Like a love letter I've reread so many times, opened and refolded and shoved into a pocket, before finding the courage to share its contents.

I want to be used like a library book with dog-eared pages and penciled notes in the margins and a patinaed cover from so many hands having cradled it.

The more something is used, the more it has lived. I want to be lived-in. For a bit, you worry that in accepting my generosity you are taking advantage of my love. No one takes advantage of me without my permission. The people that use me are the ones I deem worthy of using me. I choose to be used. To be used is to be useful. I want to be used up for everything I have (though the well of love feels bottomless).

I think our saying might go: *What's mine is yours and what's yours is yours.* My worry is not that I give more than you but that I get more from you.

cranes: opportunistic feeders who adapt their diet according to what's available in their habitat given the season and preferences of other birds so as to increase harmony. Perhaps this is one reason that many cultures believe cranes are a symbol of open-mindedness, longevity, vigilance, devotion, and peace.

You are generally disinclined to using things up. You prefer to savor.

One day I buy a double pack of disposable cameras, one for each of us, and set a challenge: twenty-four hours to use up our entire twenty-seven-exposure film rolls. The day is full, us together in its entirety. I force myself to be spontaneous and attempt effortless experimentation. It is tricky evaluating how quickly or slowly to use the film. There are no undos. What if the best thing has yet to come? What if the best is behind us? You are not hurried by these constraints. You take photos sparingly and only when swayed fully by a sight. I am fascinated by your selectivity. I, of course, devoted to following my own challenge, use up my film within the day. You don't, not that day, probably not now, thousands of days later.

—

We are at our best in our lightest moments. We almost glitter. Glitter clings to me through this year. It started on my birthday with the table you garnished. It catches in our house's crannies long after. Dots spotted in the dustpan with each sweep of the downstairs. It follows us through to the end of the year during your birthday weekend in New Orleans where we see a jar of unicorn glitter freely available for bedaubing. We immediately smear it on our skin and frolic through the day. A passerby asks what festival we are feting. There is no festival. We are the festival, the commotion, the **glitter ball**.

glitter ball: synonymous with *disco ball* or *mirror ball*; originally patented by Louis Bernard Woeste as "The Myriad Reflector." A 1922 advertisement for the 27-inch, 1,200-mirrored globe reads:

> The newest novelty is one that will change a hall into a brilliant fairyland of flashing, changing, living colors—a place of a million colored sparks, darting and dancing, chasing one another into every nook and corner—filling the hall with dancing fireflies of a thousand hues.

I have never understood people's aversion to handling glitter. I like how it buries in my scalp, the grooves of floorboards, the fibers of carpet and cloth. Sticky, invited or not, glitter is a genuflection to a past lightness that came and went from view but is not forever gone.

Glitter is a chimerical source of glimmering light. Artificially produced by filmy layers of aluminum metalized polyethylene terephthalate, like light in physical form. Once made, these particles enter into the environment, into oceans and lifeforms and the slightest of crevices and never really leave (or supposedly biodegrade after a thousand years). We want that sparkly light. To hold it. To own it. To make glitter that which is absent of glitz. An evolutionary theory suggests humans gravitate toward sparkles because they are an indicator of water. So glitter is about survival.

I begin a book-cover design that involves glitter. You are entertained by my stories of meetings with the Glitter Man and the saga of microscopic design iterations. There are weeks of experimenting with different glitters, spilled on my desk, traces in my hair, clothes, and hands. It plots my movements through the office. It trails me home. I sift it, glue it, photograph and scan it, put it on the computer and zoom in close. One afternoon, suffering glitter exhaustion, I slump my forehead down onto my glitter-dune desk as my creative director says how lucky I am that this is my job. It becomes my go-to anecdote for explaining the glory of having a dream job making books. I get paid to live in New York and play with glitter. The author of that glitter book cover likes to tell me that I do not *have* the glitter, I AM THE GLITTER.

We contemplate glitter for our housemate's birthday cake. Your Colombian friends from the town where you once lived tell of a new bakery that is selling food and drinks doused in glitter, only they do not have access to edible glitter. Customers eagerly consume imperishable microplastics because why be bedazzled when one can be transfused with a fairyland of dancing light in infinite hues? We veer past the sketchily labeled glitter and instead decide to bake a cake of gold. It is one of too many cakes we would come to design for house parties, some dusted in edible glitter and gold, others filled with it.

I cannot be certain if credit should be taken by me or given to you in the suggestion of gold. Our brainstorming sessions always blurrily culminate this way: fluid and fast, a torrential back-and-forth of ideas that ignescently interfuse. Like that Halloween when you comment that my black dress I suggested you wear could be celestial and then it became the universe. Dozens of metallic gold and glittery papers cut into stars and scattered across it. I wear the dress one night, you the next. Two galactic nights of glitter and gold from one shared storm of creativity.

Our play is a combination of the silly and the serious. A game of cards is boring, but paired with a spreadsheet entitled "Gin Rummy—Sunk Cost Strategy?" where we track timed and untimed games, cards spent, winning combinations, and other data points to determine how much of the game is luck versus skill, that is fun to us.

We like a project with thinky ridiculousness that we both can be equally employed in. You recognized this shared velleity before I did. Out of nowhere in conversation, you began setting us little mental challenges. *Count our volleys in French. Tell the boringest story. Race to the last puzzle piece. Stop the film midway and make predictions for its end. Where is that man with two totes heading on that helicopter? If you had to lead a pyramid scheme right now, what would you sell? Is that a toupee or his real hair?*

You purchase one thousand beepers, why?
To sell them as an exclusive form of communication, where you can write very short messages only to close loved ones.

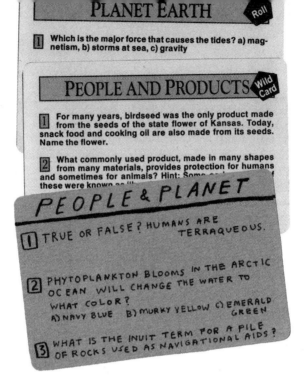

PLANET EARTH

Roll

1. Which is the major force that causes the tides? a) magnetism, b) storms at sea, c) gravity

PEOPLE AND PRODUCTS

Wild Card

1. For many years, birdseed was the only product made from the seeds of the state flower of Kansas. Today, snack food and cooking oil are also made from its seeds. Name the flower.

2. What commonly used product, made in many shapes from many materials, provides protection for humans and sometimes for animals? Hint: Some ~~~ ~~~ these were know~~ ~~ '''

PEOPLE & PLANET

1. TRUE OR FALSE? HUMANS ARE TERRAQUEOUS.

2. PHYTOPLANKTON BLOOMS IN THE ARCTIC OCEAN WILL CHANGE THE WATER TO WHAT COLOR?
A) NAVY BLUE B) MURKY YELLOW C) EMERALD GREEN

3. WHAT IS THE INUIT TERM FOR A PILE OF ROCKS USED AS NAVIGATIONAL AIDS?

It takes us twice as long to play my prized board game National Geographic Global Pursuit than when played with others because the trivia engenders too much curiosity. There is hardly a question that we both know the answer to. If you know the answer and I don't, I insist on a Feynman-style rundown, and vice versa before proceeding. If we both don't know the answer, we google until it has been sufficiently sketched out. By the end of the game, we both walk away winners in the global pursuit of encyclopedic minutiae. I love that you suggest that we make our own deck of trivia cards once we've run through all the questions. You know how susceptible I am to such intensive undertakings.

I love our inquiring zest. Whenever a query pops up, we immediately begin cracking it open. I love when we take to satisfying the other's itch. We begin with nimble ping-ponging discussion and hypothesizing based on our own reason and expertise, and fill in the gaps with some website-hopping. When we enter this state, for me it feels like electric synapses are firing back and forth between nerve cells in me and you.

Why do we hunger to know?

In a philosophy podcast episode, the podcaster says the listener probably gravitated toward his podcast because they are a thinking person, maybe an overthinking person, and they probably spend so much time thinking because they are good at it and know intelligence is what helps them survive. It's so obvious that I forget how smart we both are; there is no gap to be measured in how much our brains can intake. To have an inquisitive mind and be near someone who effortlessly keeps up or outpaces my thinking is an incredibly uninhibited mode of being.

We carry the sleuthing spirit. The unanswered is found within our investigative deft. It is not the answers we seek; it is the assurance found in knowing that we house the faculties to know whatever we itch to know. The answers are one cunning probe away, a little hacking and digging and keyword searching through records and, voilà, another question mark slayed.

There are public housing records we can access to find out about this house. Built in 1901, now worth $5 million. *He only paid $25,000 for it in 1968, cosigned by the* ████████ Before, this registry says it was owned by a woman named A████ W████ until her death. *A████ is a great name.* Agreed. *She was a documentary filmmaker. Unmarried.* A maverick for her time. What if our landlord murdered her?

How did long-distance calls work before modern technologies? Cables under the ocean, yes, but the ocean is so unplumbed and continents so far. *Laid in 1858! What impossible ingenuity!* I would have given up; I don't need to know what people over there are up to if it involves that much undersea digging.

What's the difference between a dirigible and a blimp?
Wait, what's a dirigible?

What color is the **bowerbird**? Blue, or does it collect blue? *That might be your animal form.* What's yours?

That can't be true. *But it is.*

You didn't know that? *You did?!*

I thought Krypton was the fictional planet Superman is from. *It is, but it's also a real chemical element, Kr 36 on the periodic table, after bromine and before rubidium.*

You remember what we learn better than I.

What's it called when you learn about something obscure and then you start to encounter it everywhere? Something like Occam's razor where the most obvious solution is likely the correct one.
Or the Centipede's Dilemma—sudden attention to a task once performed automatically impairs one's performance.
Baader-Meinhof phenomenon!

Now the Baader-Meinhof phenomenon will crop up everywhere.
We can't forget that one.
I know you won't. You never do

—

bowerbird: Male bowerbirds build bowers with sticks and objects to attract mates. They are engineers and artists that spend extensive periods of time gathering, organizing, and rearranging objects into patterns. Different species choose different objects, both natural and human-made. Some grind up vegetables and fruit into blue-green saliva that can be used to paint the walls of the bower. Satin bowerbirds decorate with blue—glass, plastic, flowers, feathers, shells . . .

Our planet is artsy. Sometimes you request a night of craft. Us with music and munchies and a puttered making until late-late. For me being an artist in vocation, every night is art night. For you, it's an irregular hobby but one you wish to make regular. You would never call yourself artistic, lack of experience elicits lack of amour propre, but I see your closeted creative instincts and tangy tastes. I watch you collage with a restrained conviction and consumed fixation. Art can be so solitary—I can disremember the jubilance it injects in my lifestream. But when we disappear in it side by side, it's like being granted permission to embody a fervent solitude without fear of a resulting isolation. Since elementary school, I have abhorred group projects. No one was as dedicated to the task, but also, I wanted complete ownership over my works. But with you, collaborating on a single project feels like a lamp being plugged into an outlet. I take a *yes, and* approach, wanting you to be a co-owner, wanting the *mine* to contain *you*. Even if the end result is a detour from my original vision, I am intrigued by seeing what else I can become with an accomplice.

A night of collage.

YOURS

MINE

There are many nights where you need to bring the administrative leftovers of your work home—typing reports, finessing presentations, ordering numbers in spreadsheets—and muster the stamina to be productive after hours. Asking me to join in the *parallel play* at the long wooden dining room table with my numerous commission projects, we motivate one another to keep going. Our awareness of the other's obligation and affliction allows us to push past feebleness. I love those quiet nights across the table from you, the occasional quivering sigh or joking remark as our planet rotates toward dawn.

There are long stints at that table. I buy a thousand-piece puzzle. I haven't puzzled since childhood, and never have with so many tiny jigsaw bits, but I sense a house puzzle to leisurely assemble would be welcomed. I was unaware of your longstanding enthusiasm for them—scanning eyes, swept in and scurrying until the last piece. Any pieces still attached when a new box is opened get split up before beginning. There is no desire for shortcuts. We sit placid, weightless, keenly searching, eupneic, sans souci. You do a tiny jig after fitting a piece. I have unconsciously mirrored this jig—when my new ice skates arrive in the mail; when I find a van guy to help transport a cheap plant bench; when I win the pitcher of candy corn at work with the closest guess (only four off, and no it wasn't luck, that was some tough math and spatial engineering). Sometimes the jig is accompanied by you gleefully saying *I did a thing* or *We did a thing*, wide-eyed with verve. The jig says: we are besting adulthood, or, at least, not flunking.

When we finish the puzzle, we apply glue over it to bind the separate pieces together into one frameable image. I use river rocks to weigh it down as it dries. The rocks came from a Long Island beach. You were bemused when I first dragged them into our house, though dubious of their utility. But I continue to prove their use—to weigh down tarp, anchor film projector, tether blanket fort, mark plant graves, create pot drainage, ballast helium balloons, seal kimchi, shake in dyes, and heat on back—each holding a memory of moments together. With every resourceful use, hilarity injected into our domesticity. I think you more than I needed lightness to dominate our dynamic.

Whatever the quandary, I will say, "You know what will work?" and you will say, *River rocks, of course,* and we both know river rocks are what we need. These moments of *ludus* gather like glitter in our cracks, starlit flecks through darkness.

philia

: an affectionate friendship of mutual respect
and support

As I am from abroad, you are my emergency contact. You would know
what to do. I would trust what you would want to do. I write your name
on a form without hesitation, but when I get to
Relationship:_____ I stiffen and qualm.

I don't like labels little lined spaces permit. *Housemate* or *friend* feels
empty; anything else would be fallacy.

IN CASE OF EMERGENCY

y Emergency Contact

_____ Relationship: ~~HOUSEMATE~~

Phone: (___)_____ Cell Phone: (___)~~FRIEND~~

s: _____ ~~WIFE~~

~~SISTER~~

~~SOULMATE~~

~~PERSON~~

~~OTHER~~

~~TBD~~

IDK

~~N/A~~

~~?????~~

Early after my confession of love, I tell you I just want you to be my person in this city. "My person" originated on *Grey's Anatomy* and has pervaded relationship vocabulary ever since. Dr. Cristina Yang had to designate an emergency contact on a form, "someone to be there just in case." She tells Dr. Meredith Grey that she put her name down because "you're my person." Teenage-me watched their onscreen connection intensify over the seasons. They were called "The Twisted Sisters" because, often lying on the floor head-to-head, they would confess their torments and be saved by the other reinforcing them. At one point, Grey says her husband is the love of her life but that Yang is her soulmate. I was more enamored by their relationship than any heterosexual and romantic plotline I'd ever watched. If I couldn't be your wife, why not this other powerful position? The comment made you stiffen and qualm.

What I almost forget now is that we hadn't known each other that long before I fell in love with you and everything changed. The love shortcut trust in you as "my person." Friendship love was as germinal as any other type at this juncture, and thus my feelings might have expedited a devotion well before the timeline two friends otherwise might have required to bond.

You share with me a pyramid of friendship terminology in Arabic.

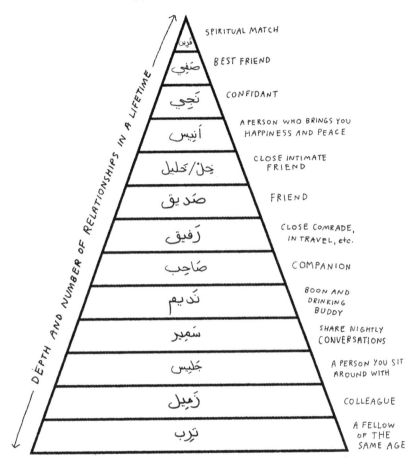

I am afraid to ask which level I am to you, not that I think you would answer, or that even if you did it would be an absolute. Some adults find partners and build families, so friendships become these packaged-up pleasures outside the constancy of real life. They have a shelf life. All of my friendships have skipped up and down this triangle as milestones impact the frequency with which we interact, most having the potential to touch its apex. My love allotments must be supple and never limited to one person.

My female friends have been the greatest love I knew before you. In most ways it is not dissimilar and in every way will probably be the most fertile source of love I will have over my lifetime. Celts described the necessity of an ***anam cara*** (soul friend) to nourish one's spiritual existence. An *anam cara* is a person to whom you expose your heart and mind, liberated from their inner confines to be recognized, understood, and accepted by the other. Women continue to dearly seek out terms like "my person" to underscore the people in their lives who will never be a partner or a spouse but hold tantamount eminence to their élan vital. I think of them as my **dingledodies**. I have collected dingledodies from every place I have ventured, both my groupies and idols; they are the ones that simultaneously fortify my selfhood and galvanize me to be better.

BEST FRIENDS

GAL PALS

BFFs

SOUL SISTERS

WOMANCEES

KINDRED SPIRITS

WORK WIVES

dingledodies: a term coined by Jack Kerouac in *On the Road* (1957):

> They danced down the street like dingledodies, and I shambled after as I've been doing all my life after people who interest me, because the only people for me are the mad ones, the ones who are mad to live, mad to talk, mad to be saved, desirous of everything at the same time, the ones who never yawn or say a commonplace thing, but burn, burn, burn like fabulous yellow roman candles exploding like spiders across the stars . . . (5–6)

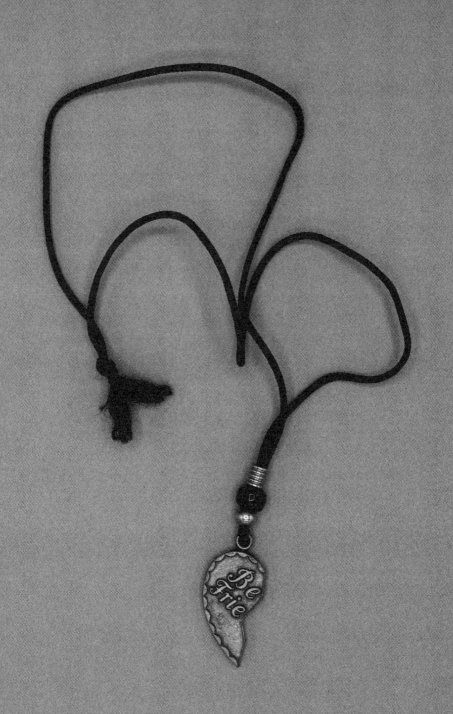

I was taught that a heart shape symbolized friend love from making handmade Valentine's Day cards for classmates. To make a heart you had to cut one curved shape out of a folded piece of paper that when opened revealed its other half—love had two equal sides.

But sometimes, those sides lived apart, like the other half of my best-friend necklace. We could form one heart but not one body. And the other half could be misplaced—sucked up by a vacuum, buried in a sandpit, trapped in a locker-room grate, traded for some jumbo marbles, or chucked with junk that had been outgrown—and there was nothing I could do about it but take care of my half.

♥

I would come to recognize that a heart is only a symbol and that symbols are interpreted many ways but most always never represent all of something. For instance, the text messages I receive from friends containing solid blocks of repeated heart emojis are not representative of forty times more love than the average loving texter but rather the fact that a four-millimeter pixelated heart does not equate to three-dimensional love, especially the love of female friendship.

In school, Valentine's Day cards were obligatorily doled out by and to every student. I loved none of them. I only had philia with one person: ██████. As a child, I would shut my eyes tight and try to summon the supernatural to split me into identical twins. I have three sisters close in age and appearance, but our correlations were more combative than allegiant. I wanted an always-for-keeps conjoining, an axiomatic coconspirator against this thing called life. A██ was the closest I've come to this. My first and only real-big friend from elementary through high school. Firsts are never forgotten. She was there for my first bee sting, first skinny dip, first bra, tent sleep, bus ride downtown, drink, concert, period. Though we are not now of the closeness we were then, she is technically my longest relationship, the repository of girlhood nostalgia, attester and partisan of my becoming. Our mothers said we should be friends because we were the same age and lived on the same street. Those are the only things we ever had in common, aside from the ensuing fifteen years of sleepovers, long summer days, routine garrulous phone calls, and after-school high jinks. She was my flume to the world. I wore her hand-me-downs, listened to her music, read her books. Her family was my entrance to what other people and families and ways to be looked like beyond the walls of my own house. We entered other worlds together, quilting forts across the basement, scripting and starring in witchy films, walking the neighborhood all day and night talking about who knows everything and nothing and neverminding the other's presence, never judged or discouraged or embarrassed. I would build the worlds, she would build the characters, we would build off the other's imagination. The way I felt about A██ established that I could love anyone with enough time spent and enough unfettered listening—when someone stays around long enough that their constancy is taken for granted—love pullulates under that sort of incubation.

It wasn't until university that I began to develop other deep friendships, people that bowled me over and extraverted my misanthropic introversion—an introduction to how loving another's soul ensured my own soul was not doomed to vagabond. V███ Z███at up front in a few of my university classes. All my friends came from those first two rows; they were the awake ones. I don't remember if it was her brilliant ideas or that mischievous smirk that made me take notice. Or was it the way she constantly re-braided her hair? In any case, I wanted to know her. We were assigned the same hotel room at a Model UN conference. We were immediate friends upon sharing that room. She had things to say, she burned. When V████ talks to you, she leans in close and lowers her voice like she is divulging the most sacrosanct secret. She cares, so much, about her work and the overlooked, cloaking authority in sweetness. She knew the story of every unhoused person downtown, spending Friday nights volunteering with local shelters to pass out supplies. She grew vegetables in her student-housing backyard and roosted amid old discarded treasures. I hadn't known compatibility before V█████—love felt through the matching of shared oddities and principles. Eight months after the conference, walking down a Varanasi alley wrapped in one blanket, we professed our mutual affection for one another. It was the first time I felt truly in sync with someone. I drank her gutsy and would follow her anywhere. I might have fallen in love with her if our time in the same city hadn't been so brief. We ran in parallels for years, went to the same places in a slightly different order, faced similar struggles at once. Our love came to settle as we did in our distant yet common states. At the last song of her wedding reception, she pulled me into the tight circle of loved ones dancing under that yurt and I spun about with her secret society of which I am allied.

A year after meeting ██████, I met ████ █████-████ while doing field research for a college course in Nairobi. She seemed too cool to be friends with me. But she sought me out. Sitting next to me at the back of the bus, sitting next to me during lectures, sitting next to me under the stairs after dinner and telling me everything of her and wanting all of mine. We were fast friends. She always gave me her leftover dessert. One month into friendship, we sat on a porch in Mombasa watching the setting sun as the tide rolled up to the steps of our beach house. She said she knew that for the rest of our lives, we would share sunscapes. I believed her. Whether it was awaking at dawn for emergency video calls across our England–New Zealand time divide, harmonizing songs scored by her ukulele on a sunny cottage dock, or a sunset on a Havana-casa balcony during our makeshift writing retreat (where I sit now and write this), we return to share that burning star of sun. She calls me *Sunflower*, I call her *Shooting Star*. She is theatrics around others, but with me she is stripped soul. Mystic sister soul and universe, believer in the empyreal. Believer in me. ██████ can achieve absolutely anything she desires, no matter how ludicrous it might seem, because she is a dangerous combination: exceptional at every art and prima temptress of whomever she seeks. She would be a glorious cult leader. She taught me how to hug—bodies pressed together, emanating warmth, long—imagine the longest hug, then imagine one even longer, so long that it stops being a physical act and starts to be prayer. That's an ██████ hug. No matter the distances, her existence on earth validates my own, exactly as it is. I know she will teleport to me whenever I need. She loves me the biggest. Maybe only second to my mother. Maybe more.

I have had many other great friendships since. Even when our paths only transiently crossed, they remain imprinted on me. I debate whether to enshrine their names here or to censor them for privacy's sake. Named or not, they are an immutable part of me.

[The following two columns consist of personal names that have been redacted (blacked out) and are illegible.]

A▮▮▮▮ F▮▮▮▮	J▮ A▮▮ Z▮▮▮
A▮▮▮▮ D▮▮▮▮▮	K▮▮▮ V▮▮▮▮ B▮▮▮
A▮▮▮ G▮▮▮	K▮▮▮ M▮▮▮▮▮▮▮▮▮
A▮▮▮ M▮▮▮	K▮▮▮ Q▮▮▮▮
A▮▮▮▮ I▮▮▮▮	K▮▮▮▮ G▮▮▮▮▮
B▮▮ S▮▮▮▮	I▮▮▮▮ W▮▮▮▮
R▮▮ I▮▮▮	L▮ C▮▮▮▮
B▮▮▮▮ I▮▮▮	M▮▮▮ I▮▮▮▮-R▮▮▮
C▮▮▮ G▮▮▮▮	M▮▮▮▮ M▮▮▮▮
C▮▮▮ V▮▮▮▮▮	M▮▮▮ N▮▮▮▮
C▮▮▮ F▮▮▮▮	M▮ C▮▮▮ W▮▮▮
C▮▮▮▮ R▮▮▮	M▮ J▮▮▮▮
C▮▮▮▮ R▮▮▮	N▮▮▮▮ A▮ G▮▮▮▮
G▮▮▮ T▮▮▮	P▮▮ R▮▮▮▮▮
C▮▮▮ G▮▮▮	R▮▮ A▮▮▮
C▮▮▮▮ L▮▮	R▮▮▮ G▮▮▮
C▮▮▮▮ W▮▮▮▮	R▮▮▮ I▮▮▮
G▮▮▮▮ H▮▮▮	S▮▮▮▮ A▮▮▮▮
D▮▮▮▮ M▮▮▮	S▮ K▮▮▮▮
F▮▮ O▮▮▮	S▮▮▮▮ B▮▮▮
G▮▮▮▮ T▮▮▮-F▮▮▮	S▮▮▮▮ G▮▮▮▮
G▮▮ F▮▮▮▮	T▮▮▮ B▮▮▮
H▮▮▮ M▮▮▮▮	T K▮▮ M▮▮▮
H▮▮▮ K▮▮▮▮	T▮▮ F▮▮▮▮
J▮▮ G▮▮▮	V▮▮▮ G▮▮▮ F▮▮
J▮▮ H▮▮▮	Z▮▮▮ A▮▮▮

A person is not a partner. A person is not in conflict with other relationships. Moreover, I don't think any one person, partner or not, should be one's everything.

Love stories fetishize marriage and pity spinsterhood. Until early adulthood, I didn't learn to scrutinize cinematic boy-girl love. I hadn't heard of the Bechdel Test, the Smurfette principle, or Manic Pixie Dream Girls. I thought love was magnetic: opposites attracting—two mismatched strangers flitting through a series of missed connections, miscommunications, flirtatious withholdings, and longing stares across a frenzied fleet of extras. I thought falling in love was about taking someone's breath away by looking "sexy." Romance as reckless gestures in the rain where someone declares their love after a brief interlude of rejection. One soulmate to last a lifetime.

The traditional couple-centric conception of happily-ever-after makes single status irrevocably inferior—missing the other half, life remains incomplete because no number of friends could ever add up to one partner. Even with more recent feminist and queer storylines in television and film, the prevailing ideal remains the primacy of coupledom.

Matrimonial dominion over familial and friendial relations seems to be partly a patriarchal construct sold to women. Sadie Graham writes of the attenuation of homosociality in such a world where sexual relationships are codified, the platonic left wayside:

> The intimacies between women, moreover, are relegated to places of retreat. In times of crisis, women escape to their best friendships for respite and support. But that aspect of escape assumes that the friend is separate from the day-to-day—a temporary shelter rather than a true home . . . Sometimes these closer-than-words, hard-to-explain friendships between women can only be described as 'emotional affairs' . . . everything needs

to be clouded and uncertain, so that straightness, above all, can be solid and certain.

Even if I know it is unsustainable to exclusively derive intimacy and love from one person over a lifetime, the images of happy all around make me demur this truth. But being perpetually single, and in the absence of the possibility of a storybook ending with you, I look for holes in the partnership construct.

Kim Brooks wrote about the unique platonic intimacy achieved through female friends. She writes of her husband, "Our emotional orbits intersected in a thousand ways every day but never exactly aligned. There was a space between us as we moved through life. Sometimes I think it is this space that allows us to stay married. Sometimes I think it is this space that makes me stay hungry for something else."

> For someone hooked up to Thou,
> the world may have seemed a kind of half-finished sentence.

writes Anne Carson after the loss of her first love. I am not familiar with the half-life of which she speaks.

It feels as though rather than finding my binary star, a reliable love for me has had to be constellated across many stars.

You and I intersect in the in-between spaces.
We crisscross plenty, but we are not paired.
Not turtledoves or lovebirds,
not swans of a two-necked heart.
Not halves of a whole.
We are each in and of ourselves
whole,
plethoric wholes at that.

ALIS VOLAT PROPRIIS

When I am not with you, I am reminded of the ways we become the same in social settings. In rooms with more talkative types and large groups, I can become reserved, hard to read, totally silent. This true version of me gets extraverted when you are next to me in the room. Maybe there is only space for one of us and when we are together, I give you my seat. We can't both be the enigma, can we? I follow you, magnifying glass in hand. If you were to suddenly be watching me, I would miss being the one doing the looking. But then, I also love feeling like the ineffable, unknowable thing, aware of myself when gazed upon. I want to feel this way and to feel someone else this way, but I can't seem to hold both feelings at once. We love someone not just for what they are but what we become with them. There is a version of myself only conjured in your presence, and other versions with each friend that I would miss without their friendship. Your rejection can seem like you are rejecting the version of me that I want to be with you, like you have determined I am unable to meet you.

I don't know when it will stop feeling like a sucker punch to the gut whenever you're dating someone new. Maybe it will depend on who I love after or alongside you. But still, if I can't partner with you, I must wish one day you meet someone who loves you just as big as I do but in a way that allows you to love them bigger back. I should want you to have all the things that bring zephyrous and zapping love, even if that might preclude me. That's the difference between person and pair. I must accept that your wins are not conditional on mine—we might nurse each other from time to time, but our growth is all our own.

With new friends, I am slower to profess *philia* now at thirty than at twenty. I overthink, or I underfeel it. This might be because I learned more of love's scale of depth through you, the love found in prolonged, consistent care. Or it might be because I have lived long enough to measure the gains in breadth of a friendship from year one to year ten.

When we talk about "us," often for lack of a better term, we speak of "friendship." Just as frequently we will instead say "relationship," acknowledging our vagueness. For semantic simplicity, I ask that we aspire to "close friendship"; you say, *I don't want to promise that, not because I don't want it too, but I don't know what will happen. I don't want to fail at living up to your expectations or have to maintain something that I can't always give.* Since neither of us has defined what "close friendship" means, I cannot know if you will fail. I hate your cynicism because it unveils all the clutter blocking fluid exchange: the dubiety that we will ever evolve past this hardship in the future, the truth about how much less attached you are to me than I am to you right now, the forms of your rejection that extend beyond romantic partnership into my wants that might always be too bulky for you no matter how much I try to downsize them. When you defend yourself during a dispute, you will try to draw comparisons to past lovers or to current friends. I will try to stop you, because we are neither.

We are almost friends, at least on the surface. And there are moments where it feels like friendship. But underneath, it mostly doesn't. What makes you different from a dingledodie? I try to establish my own definition of *friendship* to see where you diverge. I draw circles for each general point of connection with people in my life, and then for each person, I write their name in every circle that applies. You are the only person that inhabits all of them.

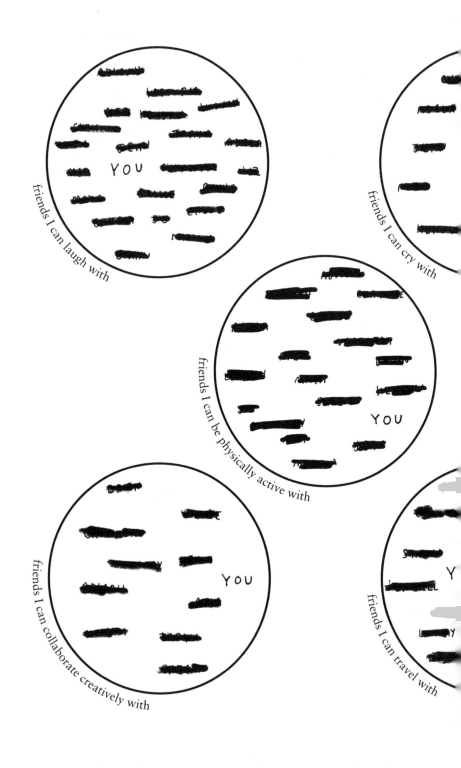

friends I can laugh with

friends I can cry with

friends I can be physically active with

friends I can collaborate creatively with

friends I can travel with

YOU

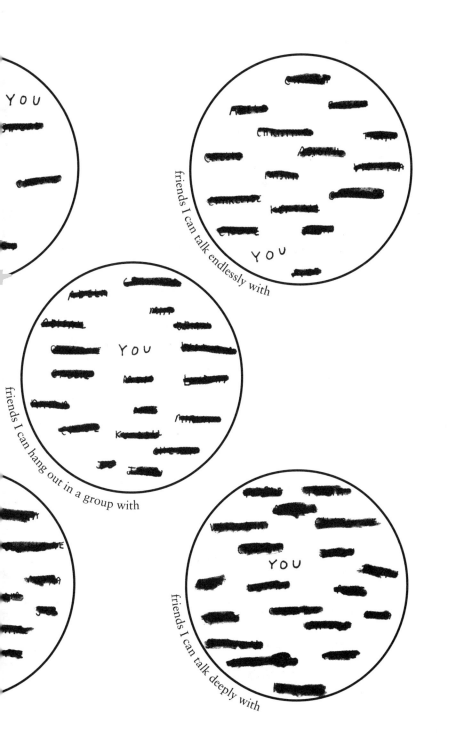

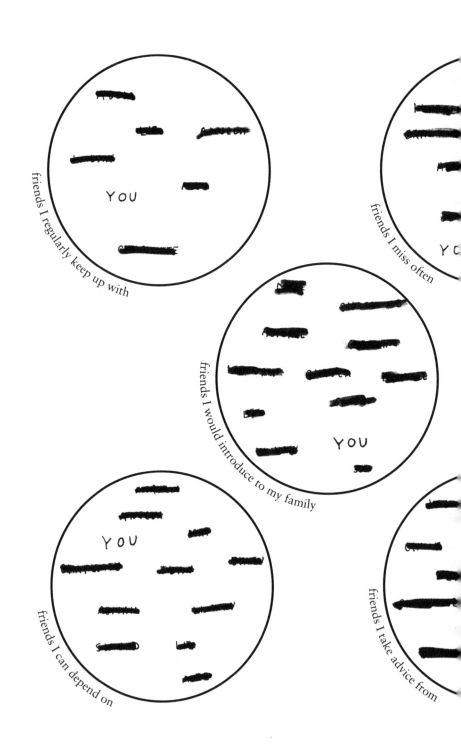

friends I regularly keep up with

friends I miss often

friends I would introduce to my family

friends I can depend on

friends I take advice from

YOU

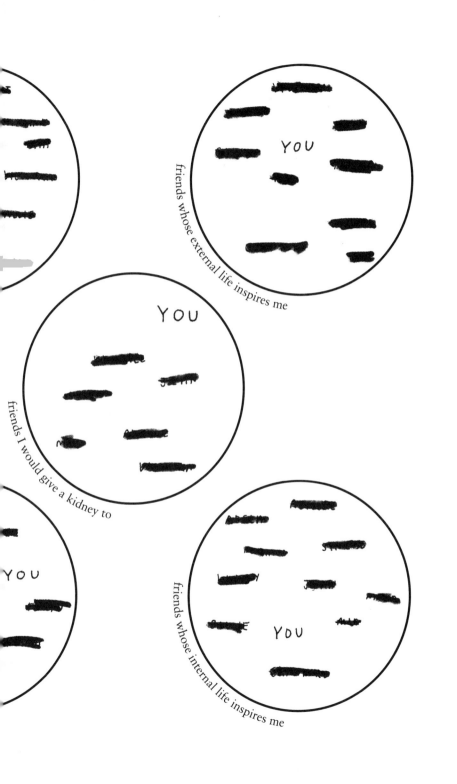

YOU

friends whose external life inspires me

YOU

friends I would give a kidney to

YOU

YOU

YOU

friends whose internal life inspires me

"The Venn diagram of 'people you might fall in love with' and 'people you might fall in friend love with' can sometimes just be a circle."

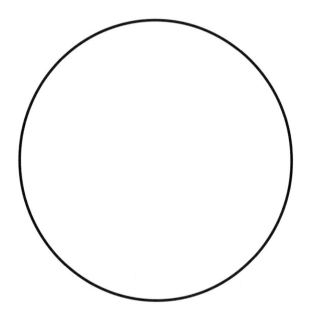

Given my pathetically mute sexual attraction toward strangers, it feels impossible to parse out the potential for someone to become a partner rather than a friend from the outset. Maybe I would have fallen in love with a dingledodie had we spent enough concentrated time in the same home. Maybe friendship is a faster fall into a shallow yet solid shared space. With you, I have not yet landed.

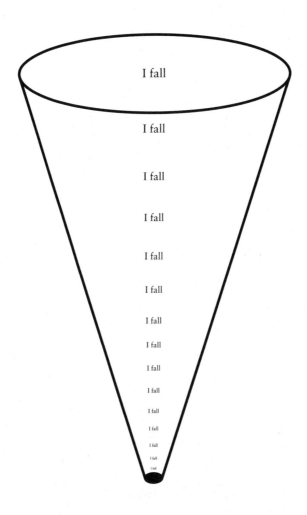

eros

: a romantic, passionate, primal desire

I am used to feeling ahead of others in most things, poised in my wisdoms and wherewithals—with one major exception: *love*-love. It is ironic to be writing a book on the one thing for which I have felt a pronounced lagging. I stop myself many times. I know which love stories get written about, and they are not mine—a story about a first love that is not heterosexual or sexual, and at times not even reciprocal.

In *The Unbearable Lightness of Being*, Milan Kundera places sex at the forefront of the male protagonist Tomas's desire for women. Women were "one-millionth part dissimilarity to nine hundred ninety-nine thousand nine hundred ninety-nine millionths parts similarity." Tomas was driven to discover this dissimilarity that "in all areas other than sex . . . is exposed and needs no one to discover it, needs no scalpel . . . Only in sexuality does the millionth part dissimilarity become precious, because, not accessible in public, it must be conquered." If true, without a sexual language, I might not know my millionth part, and may never read that millionth in you. During sex, I can feel people looking for that part of me, but there is nothing to be found.

I think my love story isn't worth telling because it's not relatable and therefore not desirable.

A close friend suggests asexual love is weaker than sexual love. No. Maybe it's more intense in nonsexual forms, or maybe it is a frequency not experienced by more sexual people, like when a person's other senses are heightened through one sense's absence. Chen believes the language of eros has become a lazy way of filing all forms of desire for emotional intimacy into a folder of sexual/romantic attraction: "Language traps us into thinking there is only one kind of pleasure and everything else is derivative . . . [relationships] are all wonderful in their own unique way. Pay attention to these feelings, their weight and heft and experience, the way they enrich our lives and how each holds their own value." Vivian Gornick wrote, "To be loved sexually is to be loved not for one's actual self but for one's ability to arouse desire in the other . . . Only the thoughts in one's mind or intuitions of the spirit can attract permanently."

I keep writing because you have marked me. I *love*-love you in the biggest, truest, tsunami-est way and it didn't need to be consummated to be fully realized. I've attempted to explain my sexuality countless times, and each listener's empathies or incredulities depend not on my story but on their own. Sexuality is as generic as a fingerprint, as adamantine as quicksilver. I write this because nobody ever told me that I could be fully realized through the ways I was made to love.

One evening I somehow explained my sexuality and my feelings of love in a way that I knew were completely understood. You understood. I feel understood so often by you without needing to belabor a point. Whether that was because of how the story was told or how it imbricated with yours is irrelevant to our story now, because sexuality is only one component of love, and it was never going to be the sole factor dictating our form.

—

For the three decades before you, my sense of attraction was puny. Then came a tidal wave of love. Of love, not lust. Not sexual, so much more than sexual. Yes, you physically I do love, but when I think of you, when I lust for you, I am not lusting for the physical. In my mind, you are not a body, you appear as this energy that blinds the eye. More celestial than erotic. Yes, I could say that I love your scent—some concoction of sprays and lotions that tarries in a room long after you go. I love the way you sway your hips when you jaunt about the house, or walk in heels and backpack en route, or drag a chair over to the fridge to reach for sweets I have left above. I love the sound of your soft, short exhales when you're focused on a task. I love the sound of your voice, steady like a note held long in a song. I love how you scrunch your nose and smize into me when we are recalling a shared funny. I love how your eyes widen when you are giddy, all piercing and wet when moved by a moment. Oh god, those pools make my stomach somersault. You are beautiful—most beautiful makeup-less in sweats on a weekend morning. You are sexy—in as far as I can comprehend what that means—when you aren't paying attention to yourself, when you are with people that you love and make you laugh. I love your physicality in a way that I have not loved the physical before, BUT you aren't what I would classify as "my type"; I wasn't drawn to your appearance, I didn't notice any of those physical details before I loved you—fizzy soul and mind. The you I am drawn to is amorphous, a viscous blue-green aurora. A side effect of which is a stinging blurred vision, because my eyes literally perceive your edges to be of shimmering *ammil.*

There is a photo of you that I took at dawn after a summer sleep on our roof. With my eyes not yet adjusted to the light, I snapped my vantage point. I have many photos of first moments of wake. In this one, the foreground is bundles of blankets, sheets, and pillows padding us: a pastel pink, a cream and blue stripe, a sage green. The background is the white elastomer-coated parapet and a nearly white sky gradating into a cloudless blue. In the middle, you are asleep, curled on your side facing me, half-swaddled in plaid duvet, arms crossed over your chest. Your lips and nose rest against a fist, only their right corners and one ear, one eyebrow, and one eyelashed eye visible.

Technically speaking, the photo is pristine: there is depth of field, sharp details, soft color washes; photographers call this time of day the golden hour. I send it to you so I can delete it from my phone because that image can't remain in me. Emotionally speaking, the photo epitomizes the physical feeling of my love. It feels like birds trying to flap their wings inside me, but they can't get out so instead I almost fly—filled simultaneously with a sense of levitation and confinement—the queasiness of fluttering wings trapped. I could stare at that photo for eternity. It is a rushing breeze cliffside, a lost breath, I go up and up and up, noise and sight are whiteness, my corporeity vanishes, me and you become a nothingness that contains everything.

I don't fantasize about kissing you. Mostly, I fantasize about squeezing your hand. Not holding it for long or swinging it as we walk as if exhibiting some sort of public display of ownership. No, just a winking squeeze and a sideward glance in times where I want to telepathically express

> Hey, hey, I'm not going away,
> I am right here. You ain't lost.
> We've got this.
> > The universe is so big,
> > > but fret not,
> > > I won't let you float away into the black void galaxy,
> > > you don't have to gulp the hollowed nebulae alone.
> See how our hands hook,
> we are meant to anchor.

—

You have a well-maintained shiny brown mane. You don't know how to French braid. Your hair is worn either straightened and tousled down or swept back in a pony. The night after my birthday party while watching a film, I ask to braid your hair.

I loved braided hairstyles as a child but my mother was rarely available to assist. My triceps would ache and my sweaty little hands would cramp as I tried and tried unsuccessfully to braid my own hair.

I play with different styles for you to preview. I comb slow and gentle through knots, smooth out sections, and dexterously warp, weft, and twist strands into patterned plaits. It soothes me to be maternal and methodical, close to you at a time when our words felt distancing. It

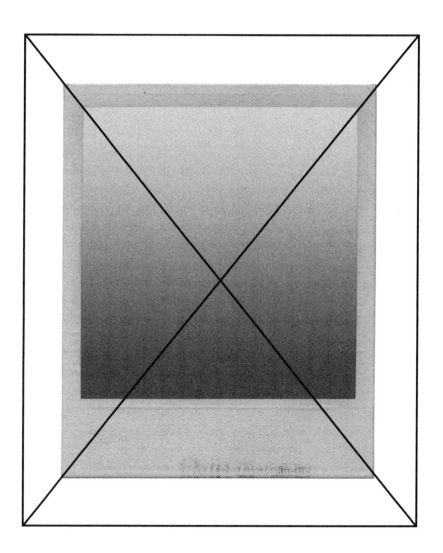

soothes you too, loving the sensation of hands threading over scalp. After that night, for many nights of each week for many months before bed, you come knock on my door requesting braids. Untied effortlessly in the morning, your hair holds professional-grade waves all day. We both enjoy the ritual and the stylish outcome, but I know the regularity of your request is amplified by your desire to slowly and gently unknot us. We can't find the words, so we find action.

One night when I am wriggling on the floor to alleviate back pain, you offer to give me a massage as repayment for my braiding. We were routinely masseuses to our mothers as children, but I had never received one. Massages are an expensive luxury to become attached to, so I resisted every opportunity for exposure—I couldn't crave what I hadn't known.

As soon as you touch my back, I am suddenly aware of how tense and *hurty* (your word) my entire body is. Day to day I woefully ignore my exterior. My body is a temple—I sleep ample hours, eat healthfully, avoid harmful substances, do yoga, and floss. However, I also fling about, heave loads, hunch over a desk for long hours, and generally stretch myself to exhaustion as I barrel through an overstuffed schedule. My body does what I say and isn't allowed to quit. But I hear its whimper, becoming yowl during massage.

Your massages offer varied techniques to untighten and allay. You use oil to warm and glide. There is an excavation involving knuckles digging through fibrous knots. Trenches are dredged along my spine with thumbs. Pain is pressed into and released out to ecstasy. The massage finishes with a crimping of the neck, a rubbing down my arms, and a supple dabbling of fingers from trapezius to lumbar that sets off an epidermal tingling from head to toe. For those minutes, your massage emulates a daughter's presence—I am permitted a break from being the proprietor of my well-being. For a few minutes, you are in charge and I am cared for.

Naturally, I reciprocate, and swapping massages becomes a weekly occurrence. Our backs require deep-tissue action, and we are equally generous in exerting maximum directed force into the other's muscle tensions. If we are watching something, we might take turns being masseuses for its duration. More often the massages are accompanied by maundering talk that pauses when the masseuse is at her best and the recipient's pained pleasure paralyzes her faculties. I love being the masseuse more than the recipient. There is a disproportionate amount of peace received from so little effort. Now in idle periods I think how underutilized my hands are when they possess such healing powers. You know that for me, another's touch is not foreplay rousing a sexual desire; the pleasure transfers from you into my center and stays there complete. And when it's my turn to return the touch, my body is not stimulated; it is emptying out the pleasure into you.

In Catholic school, touch was prohibited, sexualized, conveyed as an inappropriate invasion. You recast touch between friends as protection and compassion. I now relate differently to other bodies. I grow more comfortable employing physical touch to comfort and communicate with friends: gently squeezing a shoulder or kneecap, caressing an upper arm or back, ruffling my fingers through hair, cuddling, wrapping limbs when lounging, more hugs and knocking heads and leans into. I now hunger for physical proximity, the weight and warmth of another's body resting next to mine, to clutch closely those that I already love and those that I might want to love in an effort to replicate the way it feels with you. This sensuality resonates with me more than overt sexual acts and helps me better connect with my physicality in relation to others. It helps me better connect with you. I love causing your crumble. You always request extra time applied to that place between your shoulder blades that you describe as *where wings might have been clipped*. But I think it is where wings are about to sprout. You say my massages feel like *floating on a little cloud*. There on a floating floor we heal.

—

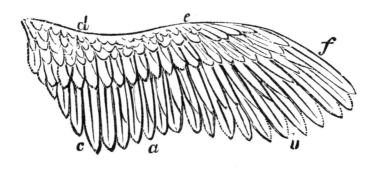

FOUR TIMES HEAVIER THAN THE AVERAGE HUMAN HEART,
AN ADAPTATION NECESSARY FOR POWERING FLIGHT.

In dating, I worry I might unknowingly self-sabotage. If I don't end up partnered, it will not be for a lack of suitors but for my inability to commit to someone who doesn't seem overtly stellar from all angles and registers. I start to feel these expectations dim over time with you. You have gaps where things *should* be. There are shortcomings that I now accommodate without bother. Things I once labeled negative or positive become neutral qualifications of your thinginess.

From as young as my memories reach back, before I knew I was non-heteronormative, before all the years without romantic entanglements, I sensed I would be someone who would not have *all the things*—that conventional tableland of outfittings and experiences that seem to come so easily to the "average" person. Before you, I had come to accept that in lieu of general pleasures, I would have particular joys. I tried not to allow myself to miss what was never going to be mine. It takes fierce concentration to ignore that which is absent in oneself but plentiful in the lives of others. But in falling in love, I realized my wants were not so quirky and solitary.

I want the compromise and companionship. I want to slow dance and camp and impress in-laws and listen to music odd to my ears and watch ridiculous videos and debate the placement of some hideous piece of art and make small talk with your coworkers and buy things in twos and plan surprises and say yes before a favor's asked and spend money in ways I don't agree with and remember when you forget and walk a pet I didn't want and try a sport I never knew and clean up vomit when you're sick and lie in bed in the middle of the day and play floor is lava. I didn't know what all the things were until I met you. Every little commonplace humdrum part in the ticktock of waken life became a thing worth doing if I was doing it with you. Before you, I loved so many things all on my own. But now there are so many other things that I want that only come when sharing life with another person. Greedy, I don't just want all my things, I want all of your things too.

Seldom does my mind run through the what-if of you requiting me . . . not erotically as much as matrimonially. No what-if will betide, but sometimes, I think of how I would respond if you arrived at matching **desiderata**. How I would be skeptical of your intentions. How I would resist but then, with how persuasive you are, eventually submit. I let myself feel full of a moment where I get what I want without compromise and everything I thought had to be gives way to reverie.

Adam Phillips says people live double lives: there is the life that we are actually living and the life that we believe we are missing out on, the "unlived life" of unmet needs, wishes, and the fantasy out of reach. We are more capable of imagining what pleasure would be guaranteed from these superior fantasy lives than we are able to imagine from gains in the lives we are living. My relationship to you straddles these two worlds. In the house, we are living out much of what I want from domestic partnership without it being fully realized through the cobuilding of a future. I don't know what an alternative version of us would look like for you, what I might eventually desire if this desire were met, what you would ask of me if I were yours. And yet, I feel seduced by my imagination.

I imagine how our lives would dovetail . . . visiting your friends for camping along America's coasts, touring with my friends through their European cities, your grandfather's furniture mixing with my mid-century modern decor, living the way we have been, progressing toward all those things we want for our lives that are so same-same . . . the compatible difference that gently nudges our growth. I imagine us on your bed in that southern sun, my head on your chest feeling the rise and fall of your breath. I want nothing more.

desiderata: Latin for things wanted or needed. In Max Ehrmann's 1927 poem by the same name, he writes "Go *placidly amid the noise and the haste / and remember what peace there may be in silence.*"

During the dreamlike teetering, air gets trapped in a rebound between lungs and palate; condensation forms in my mouth as liquid mounts up my sore throat and wells my eyeballs, brain and body languid from lack of airflow. It makes me feel so mortal, so fragile and feely like that doughy spot on a baby's yet-formed skull that can't protect itself and has to rely on others to be careful with it. I sometimes want to touch that too-tender part of me, just a hatchling letting the whole world break in. I pick the scab so it can breathe; I watch the blood prove I beat.

Love here is not what makes me fragile. It's the knowing that I won't be entrusted with your eggshell. As I am picturing a life we will never live, I am also imagining the life you will have instead, similar to my imagined picture but with someone else that you desire. I flash to small moments in your future without me: the warm evening walks toward or away from nighttime excitements, the sighs between hard tasks, the chuckle at random sights that slip into the everyday, gatherings with friends, planning the Saturday as coffee brews, water play, gardens planted. I want to be part of the picture so badly. While you are living out this picture, you won't be wishing me there drawing it with you, and I will be alone, unable, without you, to render mine.

A friend jokes there's a reason love is portrayed as being shot with an arrow: the love lodges between my organs; if I try to remove it, I will bleed out. I leave it in, and just as I think I have gotten used to it, the beloved comes by and slightly twists it.

For a sixth-grade project, I was assigned the Greek god Eros (Cupid in Roman mythology). Eros is the god of love, affection, and desire. I made wings out of cardboard, a bow out of a hanger and string, and arrows from affixing some feathers and felt to branches. Eros was said to have two sets of arrows: gold-tipped for true love, and lead-headed for lustful, erotic love—as if those are the only two forms, easily discerned and never fused. For my presentation, I sprang around the classroom flinging arrows near unwilling victims, embodying Eros's mischievous and lawless quest.

When someone you love leaves, I give you Anne Carson's first book, *Eros the Bittersweet*. You love her. At one of her readings, you become transfixed observing her kinesis. I make a new cover to replace the old dated one, first looking up ***bittersweet*** in the dictionary. Definition one: happy and sad at the same time; pleasure mixed with pain. Definition two: a plant. I look up "climbing bittersweet." Yep, a photo of bittersweet goes on the cover with a caption on the back.

COVER IMAGE: Climbing Bittersweet, *Solatium Dulcamara*
A perennial climbing shrub with clusters of orange berries and leaves varying in type from ovate to heart-shaped. Part of the Solanaceae family, historically Bittersweet and many of its relatives were called "poison apples" or "love apples" because of their toxic properties when ingested. However, their juice is thought to be "good for those that have fallen...and to heal the hurt places" (*Herball*, John Gerard, 1597). The plant can be found across New York City, thriving in dark park areas with minimal light but also enduring harsh street life. After a Bittersweet dies its bark peels into light fibrous strands. A year after its death, birds find these weather-worn threads exquisitely adapted for weaving nests.

In the book, Carson writes that "the words we read and words we write never say exactly what we mean. The people we love are never just as we desire them. The two *symbola* never perfectly match. Eros is in between," and, as you reach for the desired, "you are stirred to reach beyond perceptible edges toward something else." Carson defines *eros* as the boundary that will always remain between you and else; it is defined as a lack, a radiant absence, an insatiable hunger, a space between reaching and grasping. Love is a triangle that forms between a lover, the beloved, and the distance between them: "So that they touch not touching. Conjoined they are held apart."

In this section, I should write about the sexual component of love. But I cannot write what I have not experienced with you. Though the presence of eros was what initially distinguished this love, it will ultimately become the most absent from our story, for it is the main category that is unrequited. Because it was forbidden, other categories burgeoned as I overcompensated in all the languages we could mutually speak.

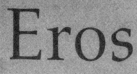

Eros
THE BITTERSWEET

An Essay

Anne Carson

After rejection, I fixated on measuring how wide the distance was between our feelings. Ultimately, I don't think it is that wide at all, just rivulets of *eros*. Over time I hope to inch closer toward being less, and you closer toward being more, so we can meet somewhere in the middle. We will never touch. Rainer Maria Rilke said complete sharing between even the closest people is impossible, but there can be a narrowing, and although "infinite distances continue to exist, a wonderful living side by side can grow up, if they succeed in loving the distance between them which makes it possible for each to see the other whole and against a wide sky!"

I smile finding your old contacts all over the house. Having spent the majority of your life wearing them to counteract severely impaired vision, they are facilely popped in and out each day. Contrarily, I wear my mild prescription on rare occasions when I want distances to appear ultra-clear. Later, reliant on the mirror, I skate the pellucid lens around my sclera until it stings pink and the silicone hydrogel gloms between thumb and index finger. Once I coolly tried to remove a lens next to you on the couch and it folded up and vanished behind my eye. Without beckon, you opened my lid and retrieved the lens in microsecond speed. I couldn't feel your fingers, but I felt you instinctively reaching a part of me previously thought untouchable. It was a sensation far-flung foreign yet intimately possessed.

In Plato's *Symposium*, philia bisects *eros*. Plato believed that philia can transform an initial **vulgar eros** into a **divine eros** (later to be renamed **platonic love**). A *vulgar eros* is driven by physical attraction, but one can ascend from the carnal to the ethereal and begin to be attracted to the true beauty of someone's soul and the eventual appreciation for beauty in life itself. This love between two people becomes the richest of relationships because the two strive to help one another acquire greater knowledge of themselves and the world.

Plato doesn't say if both people need to begin with *vulgar eros*. If I began with both *eros* and *philia* and you only began with *philia*, is it possible for us both to end in *divine eros*, or will I be the only one able to reach it? Can I achieve it without you? Must it be reached in tandem? Once achieved, is there threat of it being undone? Is it possible to get stuck between types of love? An in-between else love?

mania

: an obsessive, dramatic, jealous lust often
at the beginning of a relationship

This book exists because of *mania. Mania* would not have arisen without your response to my confession and would not have stayed as long
as it did if we had lived separately. But had we not lived together, we
would not exist.

There should have been a disclaimer at the beginning of this book:

WARNING DON'T TRY THIS AT HOME

The night of my confession, we discussed whether we should move out and away and just stop. Stop growing closer. The Internet advises this. Our friends advised this. You have briefly been me in a house with a someone like you. You can foresee an extended turmoil that I could not yet know. But we are **jamais vu**. I am not you and you are not that someone. I would be remiss not to add that our house is also not just a house but a home: an escape from the city, the center of a community we orchestrate, walls of windows that allow things to grow, three floors, two other housemates, *and* one another. We would have been stopping and moving away from a chapter of life at its inciting incident.

At this sudden intersection of love and rejection, you said this was my *crucible* period. Embarrassingly, I was not familiar with the metaphor. Excellent at coming up with snappy titles for webby ideas, you also know definitions comfort me. A crucible is a container that can withstand intense heat, you explain. Substances are placed inside and interact under high temperatures to produce something new. Symbolically, the crucible is an extremely difficult moment in one's life that calls for self-reflection and endurance. It is a temporary pain leading to essential transformation. The *crucible* becomes the coded term we use to refer to my lovesickness.

It can help to live out a crush. Feelings that seem destined to inflame one day can suddenly blow out. When rejection comes early into a crush, walking away from nascent desire can lead to a lifetime of idealizing. Friends questioned our living arrangement. To reassure themselves, they said that I would love you less the closer we got. Over time, I would find your faults, and fantasy would fade into "reality." But they were conflating love and infatuation. Reality has never blown out my love.

jamais vu: The opposite of the French term *déjà vu*, it translates to "never seen"; describing the phenomenon of generally recognizing a situation, but it feeling very unfamiliar.

INFATUATION	LOVE
☐ QUICK	☑ GRADUAL
☐ EMOTION	☑ DEVOTION
☐ PHYSICAL PARAMOUNT	☑ PHYSICAL IRRELEVANT
☐ IDEALISTIC/IMPRACTICAL	☑ REALISTIC/PRACTICAL
☐ INSECURE/DISTRUSTFUL	☑ SECURE/TRUSTFUL
☐ WANTS TO RECEIVE	☑ WANTS TO GIVE
☐ SELFISH	☑ SELFLESS
☐ WILTS IN TIME	☑ PERSISTS WITH TIME
☐ FLEETING	☑ FOREVER

Though sparks of love *mania* and *addiction* sporadically arose, voltaic reactions don't burrow in my being. But much later another descriptor entered my vocabulary: *obsession*. All three words might be used interchangeably when it comes to love, but I am only repulsed by the ugliness of obsession. As an artist, I feel prone to obsessive tendencies. There are brief periods where positive obsession can be a spectacular impetus to creative genius and achievement.

However, as soon as the word is introduced within the context of love, it feels like a secret I was harboring from my conscience. You are the only person I have ever obsessed over. I crumple in shame over the supposition that it has invaded my processing and interactions with you. I don't want to look at it. I resist admitting it now.

I sift through magazine articles on love versus *obsession*. I pick out the bad parts that ring true: obsession is birthed out of misgivings that my love will be reciprocated . . . as time passes without reciprocity, feelings of anxiety and suffocation escalate . . . I become fixated on your actions and how they might substantiate your commitment . . . I want to be integral to your life . . . I want to be so actively involved and helpful that I am indispensable to your happiness . . . I become pained during stretches without attention . . . I need affirmation of my value, which rarely comes, and even when it does brings only momentary relief from a belief that you will divest . . . the insecurity cycles through me too often; when things are tense or you pull away, I am perturbed over our fate . . . sometimes if we are really, really good, it taps into the obsessive creative in me, overeagerly brainstorming what acts of service or gift-giving or activities I could bestow upon you and sometimes do . . . it's too much devotion . . . we are a preoccupation that dominates me for a long while.

Not the most elaborate nor the most understated birthday gift I gave you was a set of rocks as useful as our river rocks but able to be stacked into a sculptural shape to display one day in a garden or put to work around your future home. A summer is spent cycling to different neighborhoods that have nostalgic meaning to you. I have never visited most of these locations, so it becomes an adventure, scouring public lands for the rocks of most visual interest and useful proportions. I need to dig in soil, edge rivers, jump fences, or drag the rocks with stick tools out from hard-to-reach spots. I fill my basket with a selection from each place and bike the heavy load the one to three hours back home. At the end of the summer search, I try combinations to select the most pleasing and stable structure. The rocks are given a warm bath, and tiny numbers are painted on their bottoms that correspond to an annotated diagram within a booklet card where I have written an essay on the meaning of cairns and listed roles for their domesticated counterparts. I think you love it but also wish I didn't give you gifts of such weight.

...........1: ....6.

...pushing around rocks since the
...ears ago. First, rocks became
...es breaking from cores, split-
...apes. Later, in the Neolithic
...rger rocks alone and together
...nolithic megaliths are erected
...*menhirs* in Europe, which are
...stones"...you know, because it
...nguish a standing stone from a
...g a stone that skips from one
that rolls. Then there are megaliths of the polylithic sort.
Ones in circle formation (*cromlechs*), ones capstoned (*dol-
mens*), those that are paired (*guardian stones*), and those
piled up (*cairns*).

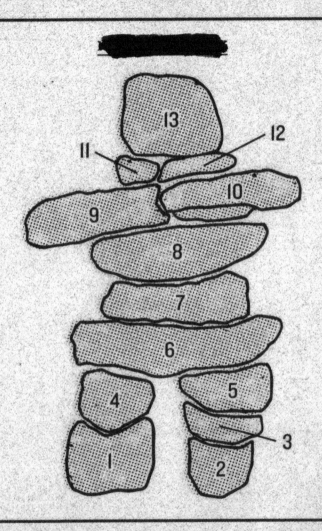

1 – GOVERNOR'S ISLAND	2 – DUMBO	3 – BUSHWICK
4 – DITMAS PARK	5 – BRYANT PARK	6 – INWOOD
7 – SUNSET PARK	8 – 615 GREEN	9 – PROSPECT PARK
10 – GLASS BOTTLE BEACH	11 – SANDY HOOK	12 – CONEY ISLAND
13		

TO ASSEMBLE: STACK ROCKS NUMBER FACE DOWN, TOP OF NUMBERS POINTING TOWARDS YOU.

HOUSEHOLD ROCK USES

1. *Inuksuk*
2. shelf decor
3. pot drainage
4. plant bed accessory
5. grave marker
6. blanket fort tether
7. helium balloon ballast
8. hot massager
9. movie screen tightener
10. disco light prop
11. kimchi sealer
12. bookend
13. door stop
14. candle tray
15. spare key hider
16. booby trap
17. kapela game
18. pet
19. slingshotting mice
20. tarp weight
21. puzzle flattener
22. foot scraper
23. fire starter
24. earrings
25. witches' bottles
26. garden wall
27. Zen garden design
28. shake in indigo dye
29. knife sharpener
30. *Home Alone* weapon
31. paper weight
32. _____
33. _____
34. _____
35. _____
36. _____
37. _____
38. _____
39. _____
40. _____
41. _____
42. _____
43. _____
44. _____
45. _____
46. _____
47. _____
48. _____
49. _____
50. _____
51. _____
52. _____
53. _____
54. _____

I had lived my whole life observing others at some distance, like a nomad keeping to my path. Your rejection felt like giant fingers snatched me up off my route and set me in a balance-scale pan opposite yours. Now my journey was one of seesawing within your latitudinal range, my weight constantly being interrogated relative to yours. Every interaction risked a disturbance to whatever distributive position our scale had last stilled on. I would feel like too much, then not enough. I tried to mediate myself but so much poured out (praise, eagerness, offerings, clinginess). The less I elicited a reaction in you, the more I felt I was not enough to meet your friend criteria. Your lack of adoration and expression comes off as unimpressed. I am terrified that I am not smart, spontaneous, discerning, noble, or funny enough. Sometimes it felt like I was the *too much* and you were the *not enough*. Too much because in all ways I am a thought-filled person; the attendance and intense exertion I apply to my pursuits and others can be too much. And because you struggle more to be organized with your time, the contrast can feel vast. I become aggrieved when I suspect my generosity might be inadvertently causing you strife, a reminder of your limits.

I felt humiliated by how little I could control these impulses, and even more for not recognizing their power sooner. I am not proud to have hosted obsession's extended stay, or that you, by association, had to play host too. Mania is not a healthy state, but it is common enough in this circumstance to be termed. My obsessive experience is concomitant with unrequited love, resulting from biochemical processes in the brain known as **limerence**.

DIAGNOSIS: _LIMERENCE (lovesickness)_

SYMPTOMS:
☒ INVOLUNTARY & INSPIRING STATE OF LOVE
☒ INTRUSIVE THOUGHTS AND SENSITIVITY TOWARDS BELOVED
☒ EXTREMES OF EUPHORIA/MISERY BASED ON DEGREE OF PERCEIVED CONNECTION WITH BELOVED
☒ HOPE & FANTASY GROUNDED IN REALITY BUT INCOMPLETE FUEL DURATION AND INTENSITY OF SICKNESS.

PROGNOSIS: _a few weeks to decades — averages 3 years_

TREATMENT: _choose one —_

1) CONSUMMATION
   reciprocation from beloved

2) STARVATION
   neglect by beloved

3) TRANSFERENCE
   fall in love with someone else

In requited scenarios, limerence will transform into healthy attachment as two people grow to understand and commit to one another. In unrequited scenarios, limerence can be prolonged by mixed signals and conflict, "hope, confusion, and uncertainty [keep] it going. The phenomenon is defined, in part, by feeling a loss of control." "Barriers and hurdles in the relationship lengthen infatuation . . . the struggle is romantic." You kept us stuck between limerence and attachment.

A few nights after my confession of love and ensuing agony, I am arched backside over my ottoman with my feet up on the armchair, head dangling near the floor. In a text earlier that day, you postponed our weekend plans to visit your mother's art studio back home, *until later this year when things between us have settled*. On your beeline from work to bedroom, you peek in my doorway to offer obligatory sympathies. I pathetically look at upside-down you. *We can't talk about this. I can't be the one to help you through this*, you say with a pained expression before crossing the hall to your room and shutting the door. I cry with my mouth clamped shut so no sound escapes.

I didn't know what this was or how to proceed, but I felt abandoned in the quest. You too were uncertain of what to do or how you felt. You become equally complicit in the manic state because of how you avoid, how little you allow said, how you will leave text messages unanswered or questions hanging in the air, never exhibiting a need to say anything in response, to be understood, share an afterthought, or reassure with a compliment. When I am vulnerable in your presence, you maintain physical distance. In instances when you become distraught or brought suddenly to tears (whether because of something I have said or something else in your life) and I reach to comfort you, your immediate response is to push me away, or disappear into your room, or say you are *still processing* before changing the subject. Unlike my processing done through communication, you prefer grappling with issues in private, in a time frame dissociated from incident. I have never experienced as much unnatural silence. It can drive me mad.

Neither of us were operating from healthy states. I could not understand your behaviors. I had not yet been exposed to psychoanalytic trends in therapy, nor had you offered an open door to your biodome. Much later, I would come closer to recognizing how theories related to trauma, emotional availability, attachment styles, boundaries, and coping mechanisms affected our dynamic. But in this year, I came to you without diagnostic modalities, believing us equally capable of receiving one another. Had we known better what "unhealthy" looked like in ourselves and the other, me an addict for the love, you overlooking the damage done, we wouldn't have stayed. But that doesn't really matter. Maturity and healing have no beginning or end, nor lockstep with another person. What we were then is all we could manage to be. life goes.

There would be months of performed lightness: our top layer appearing as it always had, spending relaxed time together, blissful bonding; a subtextual layer of monitoring the other's micromovements. Eventually I would become taxed by a collection of ambiguous intentions behind your actions, or your misinterpretations of mine, and in a fit of dramatic grief request a crucible talk. The trigger for my breaking point was often too faint to write, maybe an accumulation of texts ignored, a change in register of a spoken phrase, a tense straightening of your spine, a flimsy excuse provided for an invitation rescinded. If I had recorded a standalone conversation, a perceptive stranger might have noticed, but mostly you were faint enough to evade detection by all but me.

Our crucible talks last anywhere from ten minutes to an hour. I would share my concerns in paragraph form, imploring you to unbite your tongue, which never amounted to more than short sentences. To attempt to see you whole, I must become a paleoanthropologist. One bone excavated from each talk is later assembled by spatial guesswork. The remaining frame, absent organs, and fleshy shape needing to be revisualized with each addition.

I valued our talks for what they accomplished, but they were bigger than my mind could process alone. For a few days following each (and many days unprovoked by confrontation), I'd feel physically swaddled by a cumulonimbus—humid, ashen, and fogged. I'd sleep the deepest sleeps. You are not in my dreams. My brain would shut off and my body would take over. Mornings were harrowing. I imagine that all the particles of love and worry that course through me during the day puddled at night like glitter flakes at the bottom of a snow globe and upon rising must

A SNOW GLOBE COLLECTOR SAID
"THEY ARE A BRIDGE BACK
TO AN IDEALIZED PAST
WE THINK EXISTED BUT IS ACTUALLY
IN OUR HEAD.

IT IS SOMETHING
WE CARRY WITH US."

rush to redistribute. I'd awake in a jolt of despair, with a dizzy-headache, trembling muscles, palpitating heart, and incomplete breaths like a fish before death. I'd taste salty tears on my tongue and feel their coolness running across my cheek and into my ear before my eyes had opened.

For a few days following each talk I can't eat. I used to be slender; now I am a skinny. Unrequited love instigated a specific hunger that everyone periodically needs that gurgles with a want for more from life; that grumbles satisfaction never stays; that growls, GO FARTHER OUT AND TAKE A BITE. That hunger needs to find new fuel. I fed it with new friends and pursuits, a call to write, to date more, to chance what lies farther than I have gone before. I refused to suffer starvation; I would spurt growth. Nonetheless, the good things were unaffecting to our state. I could not find another person to love that would precipitate recovery from limerence. I have never felt so dispossessed.

As an adult, I didn't consider myself an emotional person until the crucible. I had sometimes worried about being incapable of deep feeling. But upon reflection, I feel deeply all the time, mostly for beautiful things. Negative feelings were rare because I encountered fewer erratic, adult conflicts than I had in my childhood. My family was dramatic. There were volatile episodes between my siblings and between us and our moody mother. We inherited her day's emotional state. She would throw things or ignore us or utter cruel half-truths. I used to scream hurt back until my throat cracked. I cried so hard that my face looked sunburned. I wrote obituaries to follow tragic death. I ran away and hid in the ravine hoping someone would send a search party. There were no boundaries or safe spaces. Whatever anyone was feeling would be off-loaded on the entire house and we all rose to combat it with equal force. I thought pain had to be performed to be taken seriously. I can't be sure if it was my pain being performed or someone else's ricochet.

Being the oldest and closest to both my parents, I became their intermediary postdivorce, an archivist for their marital grievances. My father found my mother to have no off-switch to her emotional turbulence, my mother found my father to have no on-switch for emotional intelligence. My mother was a drama queen, my father was dead inside. I lived with my mother in high school, then my father in college. With my father, if I was emotional, he would ask that I leave and come back when I could engage rationally. He said I was being just like my mother. Years with him leveled me out. Now when my mother tries to antagonize me, she says I am just like my father.

Until you, outside of my family, I'd held a dignified record of decorum, deriving power from controlling my emotions. I thought I was too unflappable, mature, and introspective to ever again succumb to primitive emotional states. I was naïve in my superiority and delusional in deeming it superior to deflect the reams of human emotion we are meant to face. At times with you I have felt the worst of emotions.

The spectrum of emotions that you can quicken within me in one instant is a prism, well-deep, bramble-wild. It is every emotion I have known before, and many I never knew. No one has ever cast me in such an astronomic spectrum.

Sometimes I think it is in the absence of you showing any emotions that I scan through all of them trying to pitch match.

Mania didn't naturally fall away. I worked to push against it with every incoming thought, each time digging into a groove that counteracted its lure with increasing speed.

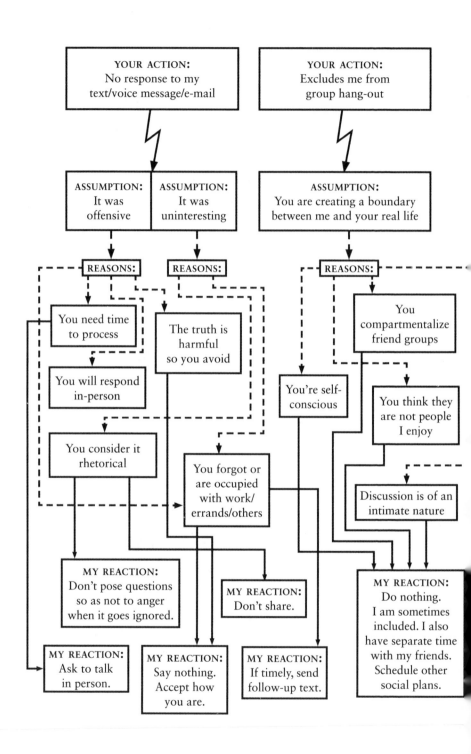

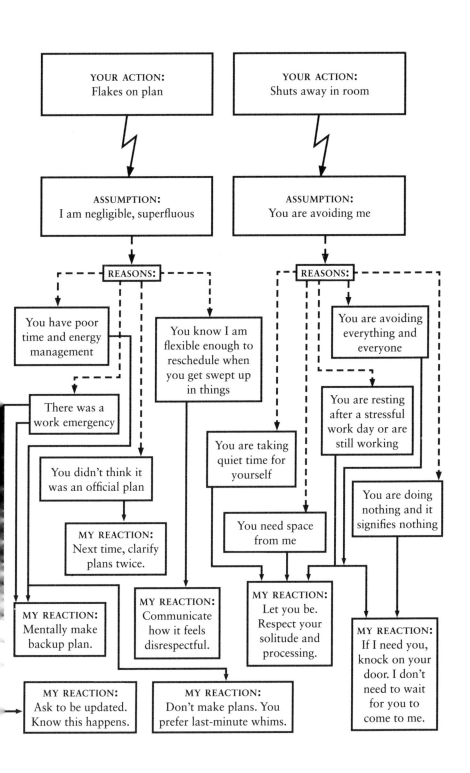

Those magazine articles reassured me that obsession was only a small part of the story of a burgeoning love: I never sought to contain or manipulate you . . . never invaded your space or privacy . . . never lied or behaved like less of myself in order to be agreeable . . . never prioritized you over the rest of my life and relationships . . . never internalized the negativity in a way that jeopardized my self-love nor desired or did anything to impede your path of growth and fulfillment . . . or, *mostly* never. Sometimes, my actions betrayed my intentions. I did things that shall not be admitted in writing or to a therapist or to you. Not ever. Things that you would never forgive. Sometimes I lied to you. But you lied too.

In the worst states of mangled mess, I didn't deaden. I awoke every day kneeling in humility and acceptance of my humanness and yours. The obsession didn't negate the love. And while both can temporarily coexist, eventually one will eviscerate the other.

—

For all my self-propulsion, loving someone else has pushed me in areas I couldn't have thought to push myself. It accentuates my lackings and inspirits me to consider alternative possibilities.

Loving you unlocks places in me that were unreachable before. Once-blinded spots become circumvoluting entrances. Intimacy requires a grappling of the self in relation to the mercurial complexities of another. Proximity holds me accountable to the repercussions of actions I once thought benign. When good intentions unintentionally cause harm, I'm implored to imagine a foreign world view. It's distressing—the sudden threat to my rightness—but I am coming to want to be proven wrong. Nothing is gained from a life assuming omniscience. The lenses through which we understand the world are sui generis, but to cohabitate we must harmonize. I am dedicated to translating your behaviors and sensitivities in order to respect your needs and limits. But it's hard to have patience for your sea of silent feeling when my sea is so contingent upon yours.

Love makes me feel like a tempest, an ocean, an **acataleptic** expanse flowing with questions that I previously thought answered about what I am and wish to become, adrift from everything I once believed safe shore.

Admiration can slip into jealousy—the pebble in my shoe preventing me from standing comfortable and proud of my life. I am jealous of not only your gifts, affinities, unplanned exploits, and closest friendships but also of your mistakes and failed relationships and emotional traumas. I am jealous of the hardships that made you, like all of our stormiest experiences that ferry us to places we could never have otherwise reached; I am jealous of where you have arrived, perhaps no more right or wrong than my own landing, just different, and maybe, too far for me to visit.

Whenever in a spiral of aggravation, I pause to remember how it must feel on your end. I give you credit for your pacification because it must be harder to embody such poise when not awash, like me, in a tidal wave of love. Once when I say I don't deserve such patience, you respond,

You deserve all good, patient, loving things.

We both do and are all good, patient, loving things.

I want to be only the best for you. We are being the best we can be to each other—hostility won't breed in our house of compassion. At our lowest points when impasse seems impassable, we remain practitioners of compassion. It is the underpinnings of my love for you and whatever moves you toward me. Passion is personal and conditional, it flounders and fades. Compassion is self-reliant action without expectation of equal exchange.

acatalepsy: the belief that it is impossible to ever know anything with absolute certainty. All human knowledge can be questioned because humans are fallible and the universe is greater and more mysterious than can ever be fathomed. We will never have all the answers, so why not embrace the unknowing?

Our reconciliations behoove a holiness of conscience like few other incidences in my life. I don't love how I can feel devoured and spit out each day. How I ooze and you congeal. I don't love the you that can't want me back, that doesn't see things in me that are as great as things in you, the things that make us sing in the same tune and spot the same trees. But the more time passes, the realer you become. You crystallize; every sharp edge and anomalous crag defines your character. We àre not the sum of our shiniest features and achievements. It is our idiosyncrasies and tangential meanderings and knotty nubs that coat our bones. That's the you I love. The meat and marrow, not the skin. And the more of your insides I come to know, the more of my insides swell love. I continue to choose to focus on that love and try to leave the rest behind.

A fictional character comes to hate his wife for "occupying an unclosing preoccupative loop in my mind, but, of course, another part of me loved her, ecstatically, for pretty much the same reasons, with profound gratitude toward her not just for her herself but also for my obsession with her, which rescued me from my unceasing progression of **unpunctuated** days, because one thing my obsession did, if dizzyingly, was punctuate." For all the loss of control over my emotions, I must admit, I too want a little bit of crazy.

Though I feel a full spectrum of emotions, most all of the time, it is not the dark side of obsession that taunts me but a compulsive desire to tell you all the ways in which I see your glow. I feel always grateful. A l l w a y s. Not grateful to have you, because I don't, but grateful to know you. To be known by you. We two knowbodies.

When googling the definition of **unpunctuated**, the sentence-use case provided is "We wished for sleep unpunctuated by the cry of gulls." When asked my favorite sound, I say seagulls. They tell me the water is near.

If I wrote down "I love you" every time I wanted to say it to you and didn't, would it fill pages of a book with neat penmanship

I love you. I love you.
I love you. I love you.
I love you. I love you.
I love you. I love you.
I love you. I love you.
I love you. I love you.
I love you. I love you.
I love you. I love you.
I love you. I love you.
I love you. I love you.
I love you. I love you.
I love you. I love you.

OR would the script morph into illiterate squiggles of an alien language?

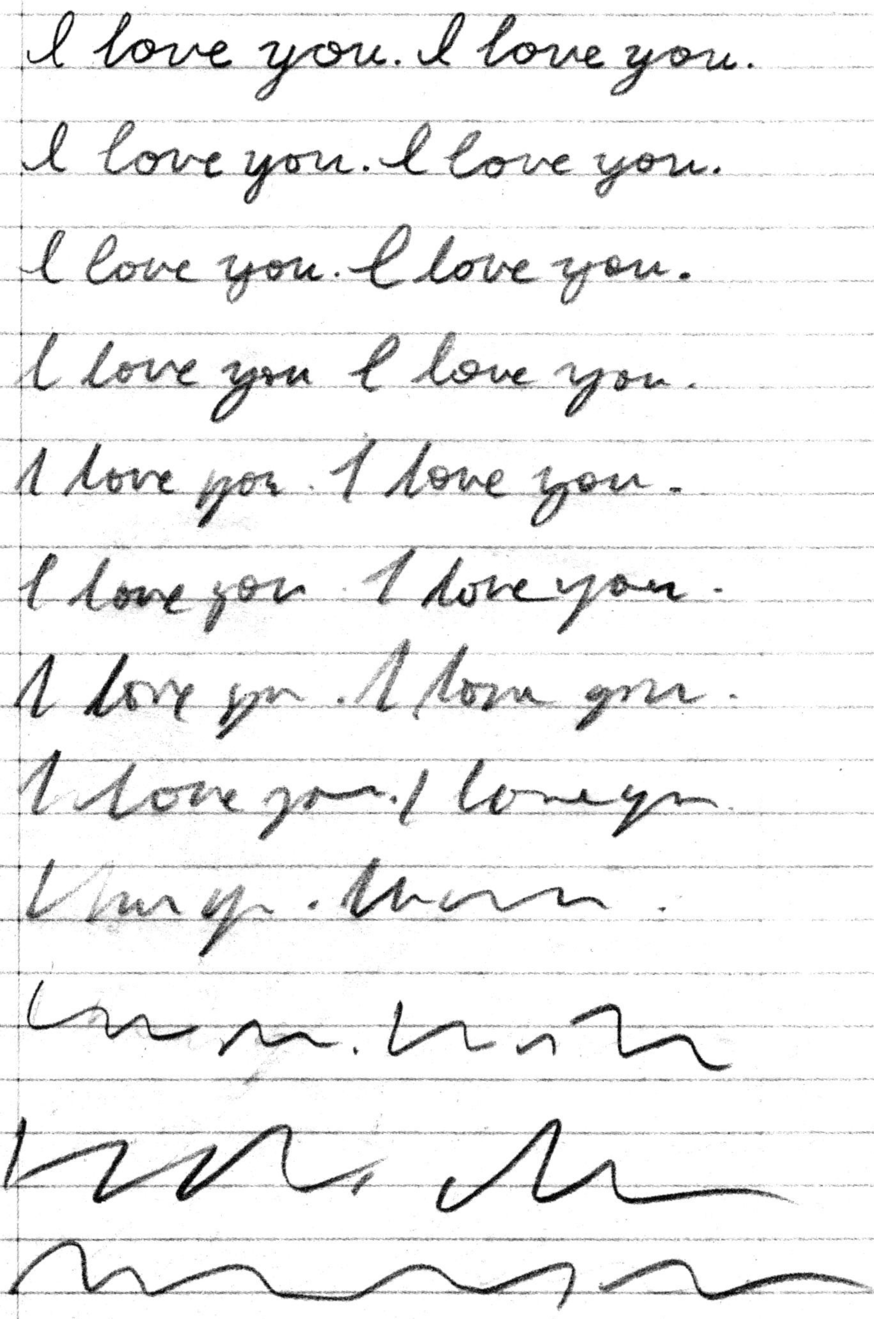

I love you. I love you.

I love you. I love you.

I love you. I love you.

I love you I love you.

I love you. I love you.

I love you. I love you.

I love you. I love you.

I love you. I love you.

In *A Lover's Discourse: Fragments*, Roland Barthes breaks down the internal language of a lover in their experience with the beloved. This language is a discourse that exists only within the lover's mind. It is a reality all their own, and can be accompanied by an obsessive anxiety in speculating what discourse is taking place within the mind of the beloved. We can never truly hear another. No matter how close the lover and the beloved are, in space or time, there is never one script, never a union of minds, hardly even can one align one's internal language with one's spoken words. Hence, love's veridity can only ever be internally verified. There is a solitude in loving.

What makes this daunting is that I can be betrothed to a discourse involving you, mind overtaken and body glutted with your marrow, and still have no more access to you, no more ability to converse with or control your discourse. We own solely ourselves.

I knew from the moment I realized I was in love that it would never be requited in the traditional sense. I knew you didn't feel that way about me, never would. I could have been wrong in this assumption, but I wasn't. I have some friends who ask, *Why? Why* don't you love me as I love you? I never ask you this question. *Why* is not one thing. What makes us gravitate toward the other and how—much—deep—physical or cerebral—chemical or spiritual—is felt not thought.

Still, subconsciously I know I am constantly searching for the answer, comparing myself to people you love, batting a bitterness over your inability to mirror me. My brain craves, instead of writing this book, to read a book you have written answering, *Why not me?* I want you to tell me a story about you, where you came from, what you are working through, where my character fits into it all. I wonder what I give you or don't give you that you want from a partner. I think about what I give you that you don't ask of me. I don't know if it's precious or onerous. I don't know how selfish I am being. My brain is searching for scrap facts of your reasoning when you mention throwaway comments about people who came close, who loved you more than you them, people who were almost right and made you question your choice in a way that I can't tell if you've done with me. I am baffled by which celebrity crushes you had in high school, which public figures you admire now, who your friends are. Does it come down to physical attraction? When you say someone really saw you, unseated you, spoke your language, what of that am I missing? I want to compare, I want to believe you are wrong, that you have some trauma limiting your ability to assess me accurately. But then I think no good can come from that, even your half-truths feel like I am being murdered. I couldn't handle knowing how I don't measure up, I would try to defend myself, coerce an epiphany, but it wouldn't change us, it wouldn't help me get closer to love with you or someone else, because, you know me. You just don't love me like that.

It feels so opaque, a flat note, one line defining my whole life.

I just don't love you like that.

I think some part of me will spend a lifetime searching for the answer. I can't make you say the things that I need to hear to make it better. I am not sure if there would ever be enough right words (though there could be more than what you offer). We could talk in circles forever, me spinning out in cycles of rejective paranoia. I express annoyance, confusion, lights and darks, but I never throw stones. I remember there are said things that can never be unsaid. I remember that when we choose to not say, it's because sometimes the truth lies not in what we think but in what we will to words. There aloud, what we choose to say shall be so.

There's almost a religion to your silence, like you had to find something sacred about this force inside you that moved neurodivergently. Édouard Glissant's *right to opacity* was developed in postcolonial conditions as a defense against the Western white world's attempt to reduce and assimilate a transcultural world into a singular perspective, but has since been adopted across political, art criticism, feminist, and queer theories.

Opacity is the right to alterity, privacy, impenetrability. It's your right not to answer me or yourself. I should learn to honor that opaqueness.

Swathed in your nature, I begin to question my communicative processing, of needing to know and be known. If we are invisible to the outside world, are we more known to ourselves? Can the unspoken be a point of connection? A connection to something in me that is often voiceless, cowering behind a shrill that gets called confident but might be a diversion. Or am I now excusing your behavior when really what you've done is muzzled me? Because when I do need a crucible talk, I am punished with your silent response. Sometimes instead of speaking first, I weaponize silence against you. I retreat behind my closed door, I ignore your knocks, I communicate through what seems like the only permissible form. No words seem as profoundly felt by you as this act. I am speaking your language, speaking loudly through the nothings. But after a while of practicing this technique, it stops being a tactic and starts becoming a tunnel to hearing your side. I run ragged my inner dialogue until your voice in my head starts talking back and light is shed on every facet of our situation and I am left dumbstruck by the complexity.

I begin to follow your will.

I love the distinctly rhythmic knock you make on my door when you want to chat, not that it would be anyone else. You knock often. Most often in this first year when I am unsure if you are checking in for me or for you. When I use those knocks as evidence that you still want in, though tinged with uncertainty if it stems from compassion or a genuine desire to hang out. My room is twice as clean and thrice as large, so we spend more time in mine than yours. I have never felt the same openness of entry to yours as you have been given to mine. Your door is always shut. I feel a disturbance in knocking on it. So I wait, on those nights when I see the light under your door that tells me you are home but in retreat. My ears plead for the sound of that knock. When it doesn't come, it feels like you are retreating from me. I let you.

pragma

: a practical, mature dedication toward another person that involves compromise and effort to achieve shared goals

The essence of a thing is in its action not its form.

—

Every time we walk somewhere with things to carry, one will try carrying the load the whole way, but the other will always insist on taking over intermittently to share the burden.

You then me, me then you.

I love how we take turns.

Whenever I embrace you from behind, one arm wrapped across your collarbone, chin alight on your shoulder as you chop vegetables at the counter or type at the table—a sort of half hug to say sorry or hello after time away or following a loss of joie de vivre—like a magnet you drop what you are doing, turn to face me, and complete the hug. The hug is never left halved, dangling unwanted. Never a hug from me to you, but a hug returned.

Me then you, you then me.

—

I love that the universe has bestowed upon you mystical sidewalking abilities. With every saunter around our neighborhood, you come across the very most ideal objects nestled free on stoops: the vintage badminton set found at the beginning of summer, one week after we choose it as our season's sport; the leather gloves that perfectly fit your tiny hands right before a first frost; the B*Witched CD appearing the same day we discover a mutual childhood fondness for the forgotten British pop band.

When a neighbor dumps a golden piano in perfect order, I brag to you about my nearly divine find, explaining that the neighbor told me it would be impossible to carry the four-hundred-pound piano up three winding flights of stairs. You respond, *Excuse us, but we'll be the judge of what miracles we're capable of.* I know it's true. We are invincible, if only because of belief in one another's capacities. It's best when we go together on sidewalk expeditions, inventing potential purposes for our pickings, splitting a marble cruller as reward for our labors.

I love how we split desserts to feel less guilty. Women feel unspoken shame over every sweet indulgence and how it might curve our frames. When we indulge together, there is never shame. We coach and advise the other on how to demand a raise, respect—all that we deserve and are afraid to seize. The dessert is a shared fuel for our separate life takeovers.

—

I love that you only eat with nonmetal cutlery. From planes, cafés, catered events, and tasting samplers, I save every fork or spoon meant to be discarded for your kitchen collection.

We both prefer eating big things with small spoons. I love when we intuitively sense each other's snack hankering. When in a waltzing whirl one puts on tea or mixes cocktails, the other grabs two spoons, and we begin gathering up our stock of containers from cupboards, fridges, and freezers (because we insist desserts be frozen). With our superbly sized spoons we scoop assorted morsels of halavah, lingonberry jam, horse-radish, Fluff, peanut butter, ice cream, and leftover homemade frostings and fillings. A grazing feast it is.

Fig. 1.

PHOTOMICROGRAPH OF SNOWFLAKE.

I love when we grab our giant spoons and shovel the snow from the walkway. It would be fine for one but is speedy with two. Tag-teaming is our ethos.

Fig. 2.

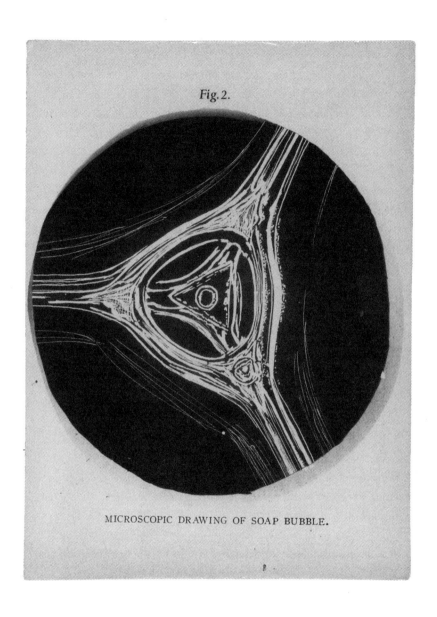

MICROSCOPIC DRAWING OF SOAP BUBBLE.

I love how you will wash the dishes I leave in the sink and I will wash yours while you cook and how we wash the dishes together after hosting a party, me scrubbing and you rinsing.

We are both astute support workers. You will send photos of plaid trousers seen while shopping after I mentioned wanting a pair. I will bake high-protein bars after you start early morning kickboxing. You will record a pep talk when I am nervous about quitting a job. I will pump your finicky bike tires each time I pump mine. You will sign up for Yelp in order to leave a scathing review after a car-rental app cancels our reservation. I will set up and take down the blow-up mattresses when your friends come to stay. When your legs feel numb or my tongue won't taste, the other will investigate online. When we both had the flu, I prepared herbal remedies and you made pho. When together, we consider the physiology of the other. I'll inch the coffee table closer for your legs to reach, you'll spread the throw blanket across us when preparing to watch a movie. When we are unwinding lights off the Christmas tree, I straddle the opposite side and we pass the bundle from my left hand to your right, from your left hand to my right, avoiding either of us going round and round. We are like a sports duo who just met but already know the playbook.

Love rewards itself, independent of external validation. It is not calcified; it is active and evolving within us and requires ongoing, alacritous application to recur. I think this each morning when I wipe down your coffee maker after its final drips, something you would never heed or prioritize cleaning. When I return from travels, its base is coated in a crime scene of dried splatter. I wipe it clean as an exercise in love felt through daily deeds.

The little considerate domestic acts we do for one another, whether individually or in tandem, have multiplied with time. Most go unacknowledged or get forgotten, but they never wane.

—

When things got confusing, I didn't break you with my fervor. You kept showing up and even when words were withheld, I remember a line from

Lady Bird that proposed love and attention might be the same thing. You and I, attending always.

There were instances where one of us would say that it felt like the other was testing them, not referring to any specific task but generally with each proposition or refusal and experience had. We would shake our heads and say it absolutely was not a test, but it might have all been an ongoing trust fall. We were checking to see how the other person would hold us. But above that, the comment revealed our conscious attempts to achieve a passing score.

"A friendship is thus ultimately defined by the desire of each person to be in it." Even when our feelings diverged, we had the converging desire to find a way to love each other that might feel good to both of us.

The first day I googled "lovesickness," I read an article that said unrequited love can be as difficult for the rejecter as for the rejected. I know in this home-based case study, it's not as emotionally debilitating for you as it is for me, but it's onerous.

Often, I want to whisper to you in a frail pleading tone,

"Please be careful with me."

Other times, I want to shout,

"STOP HANDLING ME WITH KID GLOVES."

I want you to forget about the crucible and be a free-flowing self, an unfair ask since I wasn't being that way either. I realized that in as much as you were trying to protect me and preemptively manage my feelings, I was doing the same with you. I would run through several drafts before texting or speaking hard things so that they would be presented soft, breviloquent. I knew to approach you with delicacy, a voice never

RELATIONSHIP AGREEMENT

I, _____, SOLEMNLY PROMISE TO NEVER DO ANYTHING FOR OR WITH TREE OUT OF A SENSE OF GUILT, OBLIGATION, RECIPROCITY, OR PROTECTION.

I PROMISE TO BE GUIDED BY MY OWN PREDILECTIONS AND FRIENDSHIP OBJECTIVES WITH TREE (OR LACK THEROF) AND NEVER PREEMPTIVELY CONSTRUCT BOUNDARIES BETWEEN TREE AND MYSELF THAT PERTAIN TO PERCEIVED ROMANTIC FEELINGS, WHICH FALL EXCLUSIVELY WITHIN TREE'S PURVIEW TO EFFECTIVELY MEDIATE.

I PROMISE TO ALWAYS ACCEPT TREE'S GENEROSITY WHEN IT SERVES ME AND NEVER HESITATE IN WHOLLY TAKING ADVANTAGE OF HER OFFERINGS OR ASKING FOR SUPPORT WHICH TREE FREELY PROVIDES AT HER OWN DISCRETION.

I PROMISE IN SIGNING THIS DOCUMENT THAT I WILL NEVER AGAIN FEEL RESPONSIBLE FOR ANY PAIN OR SUFFERING THAT MAY OR MAY NOT BE EXPERIENCED BY TREE AS A RESULT OF THIS ABNORMAL FRIENDSHIP THAT SHE HAS WILLFULLY ENTERED INTO AT HER OWN RISK.

I PROMISE I WILL BE HONEST IF AT ANYTIME I FEEL I CANNOT UPHOLD THE COMMITMENTS SET FORTH IN THIS DOCUMENT AND TRUST THAT TREE WILL NEVER AGAIN MENTION ITS CONTENTS OR DOUBT MY ADHERENCE TO THEM.

SIGNATURE (███████)   SIGNATURE (TREE)

raised, accusations traded for curiousness. I would overcommunicate all possible concerns you might have been stomaching alongside possible counterarguments and conciliations as if providing consent to your silence. Four months in, we were still tiptoeing across a sheet of smashed glass, avoiding the cracks but inadvertently shattering more with each step. We were expending far too much energy deciphering the other's underlying impulses and trying to curtail our own. So I draft this contract, telling you I wrote it because I don't want to be a source of guilt in you.

You are sitting on the floor in my room, knees up, back against the closed door. I am sitting a few feet away. I pass you the spiral notebook that I had begun journaling in to process this following my birthday. Each entry's date was paired with a number counting up from then. I had reached the end. Page 140. Titled "DAY 116." The contract uses this last sheet. I want it to close the autopsy phase of us.

While you read, I stare mostly at the floor. I scratch at the waxed grain and run my index finger along jagged seams.

In good spirits, you smile, noting how authentic the legal language sounds. Then you are quiet for some minutes, eventually sliding the notebook across the floor and back to me. You say in a tone of genuine endearment for the gesture, *I appreciate your recognition of my feelings in this SO much*, and, after a slight *enh* sound of vocal cord friction (you make this when there's something that you must say but really don't want to): *I can't sign this.*

The contract seems so foolish now. I wanted to clinically excise romantic love from our dynamic, apathetically tweeze it out like that tiny plastic "broken heart" piece on an Operation game board. You had been conscripted as operator to a love that wasn't floating in a cavity but was the electrified wire looping every part of me, becoming a fire-red zap each time you approached the obviously inoperable.

Inchmeal, I am learning that our intentions are not stable, not mirrored. Neither are our issues or conditions within which we feel safest. We don't struggle in the same moments or react negatively to the same stimuli. Our core selves might be related, but they are plastered in many life layers that can hamstring our ability to modulate ourselves the way the other ideally wants. The resemblance of our states waxes and wanes. Sometimes we are so joyfully close. Then one or both of us reaches our most unwell extreme and every expectation must be adjusted, suspended, abandoned.

I couldn't be the sole arbiter to a relationship agreement. It wasn't disappointing. By not signing that contract, you bound us to a commitment of *pragma*'s negation. *We* were the shared goal. And there would be no Rosetta stone chiseled with the key to achieving that goal. It would become a regular renegotiation of lines drawn and the spaces between to espouse the other's suffering, but also, the other's love.

—

Though your biography remains patchworked and holey, you have disclosed a substratum of the sticky, the chagrin, the violating—betrayals done by or to you. I have become part of this underbelly. There is unlikely another person incidentally more harmed by you than me. I have experienced you callously obdurate, frantically evasive, negligent, selfish. The same can be said of the muddy nature you know and have received of me. In Catholicism, **grace** is defined as a God-given gift, a little bit of godliness that allows us to participate in a life of forbearance and love, to heal and sanctify our souls. Eileen Myles, long after they had forsaken the church, said, "I knew how god felt, being fully occupied." Perhaps the concept of God shaped me. While neither of us are theists now, we have granted one another a godly grace. In psychology, a pillar of healthy relationships is *unconditional positive regard*—respecting and supporting someone regardless of what they say or do, nurturing empathetic space for constructive growth without fear of judgment. When one's flaws are intimately sowed at the feet of another, and both remain unmoved, one is anointed whole. I carry that acceptance with me.

You hold the power to regulate our climate. You could be hot then cold. I was overly sensitive to the shifts. I am still acclimatizing.

I am ferociously vulnerable, you can be diametrically closed. When asked what we'd hypothetically want to happen to our hypothetical diaries after we die, you say *burn them* as I say *read them*. At no point ever do you want your private thoughts to be seen by anyone. By *read them*, I mean that anyone can publish them, broadcast their contents, read them now, right in front of alive-me if that serves them. I read over your shoulder an article on the writings of Lucia Berlin, "fear that everyone will see her shame is less than her fear that no one can see her at all." I ask and you confirm an opposing fear. I, the artist, align with Berlin. You carry on reading, saying nothing more.

The hurt we cause the other is placated as our instinctual differences are gradually grasped. Having not shied away from the situation, we are both walking through a fire. But I walk just as I am, skin burning off, guts below exposed for all to see. The walk is excruciating but unflinching. All I need are my brain, heart, and eyeballs; the rest will regenerate. You, by contrast, enter with a full suit of armor. You remain intact— private and unseen, but it is harder to bend or maneuver. The walk is leaden. But I sense underneath is a self made of marshmallows and toothpicks that needs the steel casing to keep from turning to ash. It's the way it must be. Regardless, we stay walking through a fire that most would have run from. Along the way, we pretend to believe the self— cauterized-me and armored-you—that the other is attempting to present as fortified against the fire. We both willed these versions of ourselves into existence, and, a lot of the time, it worked.

So, I blame you and forgive you at the same time.

I blame you for the months when you were sealed off—closed to talking about what I was going through, unwilling to be honest about how it made you feel. I blame you for the double rejection of romance and friendship resulting from your inability to use words to reassure. I blame you for making me feel wrong, out of sync, and distrustful of my intuition.

I forgive you because you don't effuse sentimentality like me. You don't warm nimbly, you didn't have a childhood that desensitized you to the flames of conflict and confrontation. I forgive you because I know more now of how this experience was triggering for you. For me this love was the first of its kind, but for you it carried hauntings of past implosions.

I blame you for not trusting what I could handle, for not discerning my difference to them.

I forgive you for trying to protect me from the fire, and for valuing your self-preservation enough to take precautions to protect yourself.

Sometimes your behavior nicks my brain and I quaver upon the invitation to distrust you: I am convenient until one day I am not; you'll never hold more space for me; I am wasting love on someone who sees no value in it; I have mistaken Stockholm syndrome for love. A whole case could be made around these nicks. I could fretsaw the evidence in this book slantwise and sculpt a story of your impending betrayal and my pathological embellishment. Some days it would be a more bearable truth than having to watch a love fly away. But I am not prone to doubt. Even if my brain wants to, my heart will not abide. In me, hope and trust are a priori, and they auto-renew. I won't make red flags of your vices. I am becoming someone who can love without perfection or fixity.

—

178

The faucet on our claw-foot tub had long been leaky when the cold handle finally stripped its stem to the point of futility. I had finished showering but couldn't turn off the water, the faucet handle spinning without grip. I knocked on your door to see if you knew a fix. You had weaseled the water off after great effort earlier in the day but were now unsuccessful. Squatted down next to the handle while I sat on the toilet seat we calmly discussed what to do. Definitely the landlord would have to be called, but he lived in Woodstock, so that was not an immediate solution to the water drumming out. Our ground-floor neighbor could turn off the main line, but then we would be without all water. Discovering that horizontal force exerted on the handle stopped the water, I went and got a thick rope and a collapsible T-shaped metal laundry-drying rod. With one end of the T's crossbar bent down in front of the handle, the stem of the T and the other end of the crossbar leaning against the backside of the tub, I wrapped the rope around all parts. But it wouldn't tighten enough. Watching this, you fetched a large umbrella and a stick, to reach along the inside of the tub, applying pressure within. I hadn't thought of that. Nothing was long enough on its own. I retrieved a massive metal pot, which, combined with your stick, spanned the inner extent. There was slippage. I requested some of your resistance bands. Wedging them between the handle and the pot, the pot and the stick, and the stick and the tub provided ample tension and grip to stay in place. The water ceased.

We cry-laugh, impressed by our improvised engineering, humored by the wacky scene. This photograph symbolizes what we were in the house, a muddling through making do by two, precariously keeping the flood at bay with whatever makeshift tools and successive maneuvers our collusion catalyzed.

I rarely confide our alchemy to friends. I worry that if I were to speak the magic aloud, today's might dematerialize and never recur. I wish to capture all our secrets so that I can keep them for the tomorrows after we run out. In second grade, we were only permitted to write in pencil until the teacher evaluated our script to be neat enough to graduate to pen. That's what our *pragma* feels like, a relationship penciled in, able to be erased, copied out page after page, hoping to be granted indelible ink. *Pragma* is a love found in an enduring commitment that is proven only with time. More time than the year that spans this tub. Blank pages must be left in this section for the future to fill, because our relationship agreement of *pragma* might only be ratified through future decades of committed refusals to sign.

....
....
....
....
....
....

storge

: an enduring natural bond between a parent and
a child or individuals who build memories, trust,
and emotional connection; a form of home

For Christmas, you gift me a blue hippo figurine from the Met Museum Store. It is modeled after a faience statuette ("William" the Hippopotamus) in their collection. You were referencing a Canadian television PSA that I showed you from my childhood. Shot like a nature documentary, a narrator describes the habits of the house hippo as doctored video footage shows a mouse-sized hippo roaming indoors, leaving peanut butter footprints after snacking on toast, swimming in the dog's water bowl, and building a soft nest out of lost mittens and dryer lint. A child viewer dangles in verisimilitude all the way through to the end when the Concerned Children's Advertisers warn that just because something looks real doesn't mean it is. House hippos are not real. Rewatching the PSA, I lick at the desire nine-year-old-me felt of wanting it to be true, wanting then and now to believe there are still things I don't know, that I can sit wonderstruck and humbled even in the commonness of my own home.

And I do,
with you,
my fellow house hippo.

—

I notice myself drawing comparisons between my yearning for you to that of a child to her mother, or a mother to her child. While I no longer desire my mother, it might be an umbilical association when I first learned to reach for something to keep me alive.

Love, in the form of attachment to those that consistently give us care and affection, is the earliest and most necessary emotion we learn. My family said *I love you* enough that even when they were hateful, I never doubted it was underscored by love, or, at the very worst, and most often with my sisters, a love-hate. I learned a parent's love was undying from the children's book *Love You Forever* as read at bedtime by my dewy-eyed mother. She said having us was like having phantom limbs—these

Dear Tree

It is not your folt
I know how it feels you
do not half to be sorry

I Love so munch!
You deffently are I good
sister if I ever said anything
or if I do say something mean
I don't mean it.
from Paytonn

I Love you!
I LOVE YOU!
XOXOXOXO

chunks dismembered from her body but remaining a part of her somato-sensory nervous system.

My childhood was one of wanting to be sent away: to overnight camps, boarding schools, trips abroad, horseback-riding ranches—places where a new family might arise, where passion, felicity, and even struggle were embraced collectively. I wanted to be orphaned and adopted into a home on TV that looked so ordinary and happy in its acquiescence to daily routine and custom.

Our family never operated as a unit. My parents were allergic to tradition, community, and each other. Coming from homes of overstretched single parents themselves, they were not taught to micromanage their children. They took us in shifts. If my father wasn't working, he would be with us and my mother would go out. Rarely did both attend a mandatory school event; both would have preferred to skip them. Seasonal holidays were driven by social guilt, to which my parents responded with minimum action. They didn't care for special meals, decorations, or marking milestones. I could count how many times I saw them socialize with friends. Hosting was stressful for my mother and of little interest to my father. It might have occurred, but I haven't kept memories of the six of us together in a conjunctive gladness. Self-sufficiency was the prescribed treatment for every ailment. We were a house of free agents, dismembered limbs without articulated joints collectivizing our movements or a corpus coagulating our loves. My parents loved us from a distance.

On an 8mm cassette tape from age two, my mother asks me, "Who loves you?" I am assisted in naming everyone in our extended family, no more than ten in total. And I learned to love them back. I said *I love you* through their deficiencies. I said *I love you* through divorce and depression and disappointments felt in the smallness of a childhood absent of financial resources, family vacations, festivities, and extracurricular activities. Susan Sontag wrote in her journal, "Every act is a compromise (between what one wants + what one thinks is possible)." I got love in the form they offered up. I loved them because they were all I knew and all I had. But my needs made themselves known in adulthood, to find people that wanted to build something together.

More than anything, I want to embroider a home. In Welsh, *hiraeth* is defined as a feeling of homesickness, of a longing or wistfulness for a home that you cannot return to, was never yours, or may have never existed. Home can be found in many people, places, and things, which moves us to search for a home, even if we never had one. It's a reassuring word because being aware of a vacancy is proof of an existence somewhere to which we are capable of belonging. Home could be a fantasy dreamed into reality. Once we leave our first home, it doesn't make much difference what of a home was left behind because now we are matriarchs in the making. If we're lucky, we'll find people wanting to slow enough to build something of a home with us.

Love is not this permanent state of being; it is a flaring force that can briefly feel like a fusing of the "boundaries between you and not-you," and the only "difference between the love you feel with intimates and the love you feel with anyone with whom you share a connection is its sheer frequency," says researcher on emotions Barbara Fredrickson. She found that love consists of micromoments of positive resonance between any two people who connect in a moment. A study involving fMRI scans documented a mirroring of brain activity that can occur during an exchange between two people—talking, listening, laughing, eye contact, forms of affection—many sips of love become a love-filled life.

A home is the concentration of those micromoments. Generations before prepared us for the externalizing and concretizing of a home through marriage, mortgages, and children, but not for this time between starting and settling, where I would live with housemates without any legal or genetic ties binding us together. It doesn't feel like an in-between-making-do-waiting-for-something-better. It feels as legitimate. The four of us became the corners adjoining walls to roof. I have lived alone before, deprived of love found in community. I don't want to return to that. I want to live with people forever. There is a love in the way my housemates watch over one another.

Love is a housemate that gifts me an old copy of *Bäume* with Post-it
    Notes annotating every German line into English because there is
    no official translation and she knows my reverence for Hermann
    Hesse's tree thoughts.
It's the squealing chorus we let out when we spot a housemate running
    the marathon and she sees us with our homemade sign telling her
    to RUN, and she does, right over to us all jumping up and down
    in pride and she runs on faster and we feel like we're running too.
Love is taking turns trying to open a tight-lidded jar until the most
    persistent grip pops it open.
Love is switching ice cream flavors with me when I regret my
    selection, and eating off one another's plate or drinking from
    the other's glass without needing to ask.
It's reading an entire thesis, editing a job application, or nightly
    quizzing in the lead-up to an exam.
Love is a long, warm, tight, rocking hug that is held until breathing
    patterns align, mine shallowing, briefly levitating grief off my
    chest into this shared breath.
Love is a someone who tries to deconstruct anatomical diagrams to
    quell concerns that a menstrual cup got lost in my uterus;
and blasts "Cabaret" through my shut door because *What good
    is sitting, alone in your room?*
It's a someone who paints my nails with avant-garde decals;
and accompanies me to events guaranteed lame;
and spins me around before a hit to my birthday piñata;
and fixes the ribbon in my typewriter when I want to smash it
    in frustration;
and finishes weaving my tapestry when I lose momentum;
and saves me from a mansplainer at a party;
and takes candid photos that capture my best angles;

and tells me which expired foods are safe to eat;
and gives me the batteries from her speaker so I can use
my bike lights;
and leads a sacred fire ritual when I need healing;
and returns a library book when it's forgotten;
and replaces the cherished umbrella she lost of mine with the
swankiest British-made, steel-shafted, fiberglass-ribbed,
double-canopy doppelgänger.
It's a someone that stands patiently next to me at a flea market where I
am insistent on examining every junk scrap in an overflowing box;
and helps thread the bobbin on the sewing machine and decrypt the
instructions on the new convertible handsaw and shows me the
wire-cutter portion of pliers that I never knew existed.
Love is lying about pipes bursting to leave work early and tour a
recycling facility or trash museum or rooftop garden, because
those are the kinds of rebels we are.
It's snaking the toilet to stop a rainstorm in our foyer;
and enthusiastically complying with the chore chart, because we all
love the clean, and many housewives make for breezy housework.
Love is indulging in just one more round of Bananagrams;
and endeavoring to make dumplings, and pasta, and roulade from
scratch, each chef contributing their slice of food-show expertise.
Love is a housemate that kills the cockroach I left under a glass;
and opens another window so my spray-painting doesn't kill
our brain cells.
It's taking the blame when I exceed my quota of broken dishware;
and rubbing sunscreen on that one spot between shoulder blades that
I can't reach.
It's donating old clothes to be repurposed in the other's wardrobe
and spooning heavy-dose medicine when the fever hallucinations
take over.
It's a text sent before or after something scary to see how I'm faring,
signaling that someone is ready to scoop me back up whole again
no matter what.

Home can be a cradle made up of those who know how to love.

We take turns being hype girls and therapists, sisters, mothers, daughters, teachers, and pupils, propagators of compassion, connoisseurs of conversation.

We who observe and listen—

listen to every rambling, repetitive, random, neurotic thought that might arise from any silly or stupid or tragic event that can be packed in a single day.

Love is choosing to be here. To make rules and break them. To lighten loads. To show up and check in and share and make things festive and hygge and home.

And that is only a brief list of what they have done for me. Identity can be formed through acts of service, through modifying behaviors to relate better to others and the **fluid mosaic** boundaries we hold. If I squeeze out all that I have to offer to my microworld, it's not selfless, it's

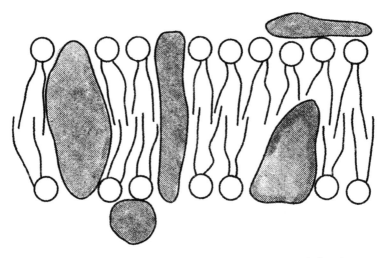

fluid mosaic: the boundary of a cell membrane that protects its inside from its outside selectively, allowing particular particles to flow through it by sensing what is toxic or nourishing and regulating its interactions accordingly. Like a smudgy outline of a self retained without sharp definition, a self influenced by its purlieu but not lost to it. A choice that is made about what we allow to influence us.

self-sustaining: the more I give, the more others give, in a feedback loop, and a centripetal force builds wherein it becomes impossible to separate the love of home from the love for its members.

This home of housemates penetrates my self-definition. It doesn't make me feel smaller or defensive of my uniqueness. The greater the sense of community I feel, the more I come to sense myself.

—

This openness and intimacy of home is most robust between the two of us. Well beyond what I ever achieved with my territorial sisters.

Brian Blanchfield writes that one's peripersonal space is not a matter of "valuation but rather instinct, to protect not what is most precious but what communicates itself as an extension of the self: the loosest, heaviest things in one's near space. That which is most susceptible to detachment from the intact integer one feels one is." This home and its contents have become an extension of my body.

Aside from a few throughout my childhood, I have never spent as much time with another person as I have with you; no one has watched me as closely or listened to me so frequently; no one knows more of me; I know no one more than you; and still, I don't tire of your company.

Because this was my first time, I wonder if I am capable of falling in love another way but in the dilating attachment of home. Is this how love works in me? I know that our story would not have been performed without this stage. I also know that if this home had felt like eternally enough for you, I wouldn't be writing this story.

You want a home headed by a romantic couple. **Amatonormativity** is the bedrock of our society that has either pressured or primed us to desire a lifelong monogamous, sexual/romantic marriage.

A new queer friend shares a social media post:

> In my growing queerness, I've learned the grand importance of platonic relationships. Growing up, I was shown how friendships get pushed aside when you meet your partner . . . To me, heteronormativity is more than just the idea that being straight is normal. It dictates how we show up in relationships, who we spend more time with or give more energy to, where our loyalty is supposed to lie and who is supposed to fill all of our needs . . . Since being in queer community, I've seen all of these ideas flipped upside down . . . Queerness is not perfect. You don't come out and automatically change all of your ideals or practices. For me, it has happened (and continues to happen) slowly. Queerness is more than my s-xual and gender identity; it expands my mind on the possibilities of how I want to live, how I want to relate to those around me, and how I understand intimacy and community.

To be *queer* is to reject definition by replacing labels with a question, says activist Shon Faye. The post changed my understanding of my own queerness. I was raised in a time and place that wasn't for me. I come with amatonormative wants, but I experience love beyond that structure, despite not yet living among people that embrace an expanded vision for togetherness. In the years since, I have become acquainted with more queer community that operates by this fluid code, but right now neither of

amatonormativity: coined by philosophy professor Elizabeth Brake as
the widespread assumption that an exclusive, romantic, long-term coupled
relationship is the shared goal that everyone is or should be seeking above other
relationship types

us are members. How much easier would it have been if we were? How much happier could I have been single if I lived with queer housemates in a queer world? I think I might one day find out, and when I do, I will be ready to love it totally.

Through queer theory (which itself resists academic delineation), I learn of the **queerplatonic** relationship, coined by the asexual community to describe a connection that queers the essence of close relationships that are not sexual or romantic but that hold an emotional intensity and intimacy beyond friendship. Queerplatonic relationships are allowed to be whatever the people involved make of them. From the outside, we might appear to be queerplatonic, but on the inside we are two people who understand each other in another time/place/society. We are not equal stakeholders to queerness. It is me investigating these alternative realities and opening to the possibility of folding into them, or needing to open because of how I am built. If you have conducted your own investigation, you have not shared your findings. Right now, what we want and from who is discordant, in flux, uncomforted by external definition.

—

Agape, philautia, ludus, philia, eros, mania, pragma, storge.
We are not a mere one of eight.

In Hungarian, "I love you" is one word—**szeretlek**. The object and subject cannot be excised from the love, indivisibility inherent to its quality.

I. love. you. But I realize that in this experience, though love is universal, we are not. And it is not the *love* that needed definition, it is the *you* that I am defining in *me*. The *I* with *you* is the only word for what *we* are.

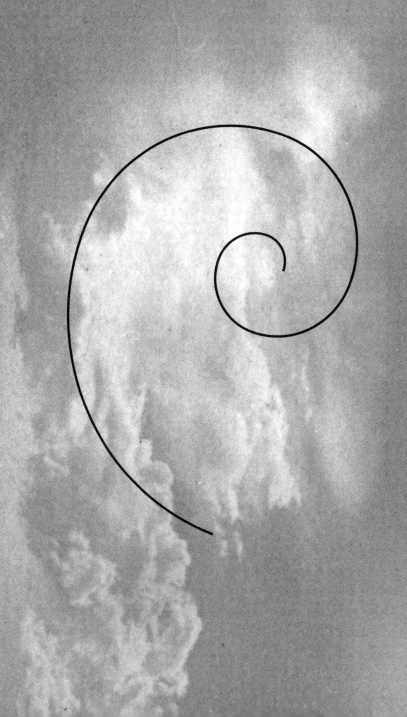

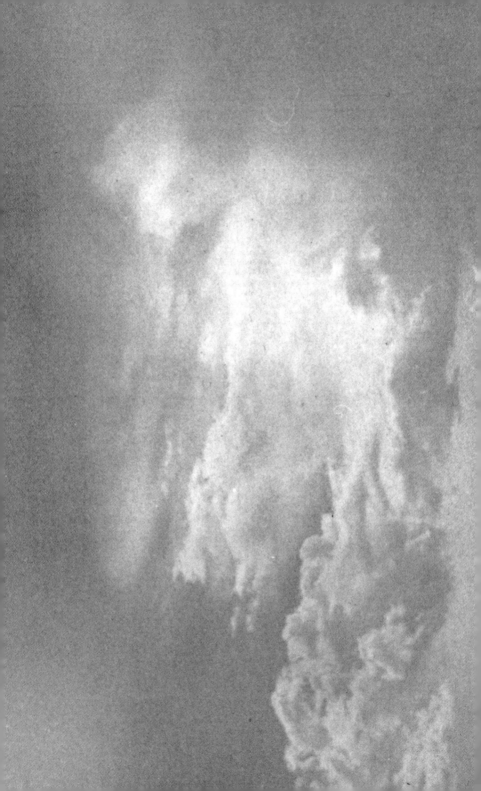

I find a Venn diagram of four overlapping circles of love types.

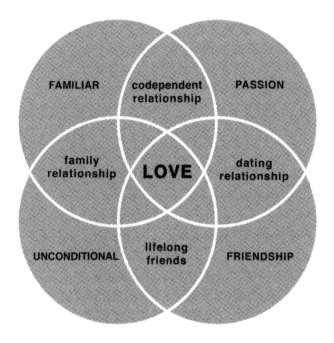

Automatically I want to smush the disparate parts into some sort of figurative Silly Putty.

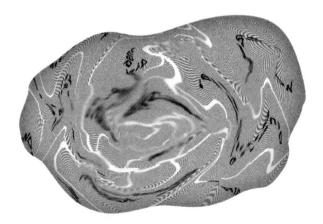

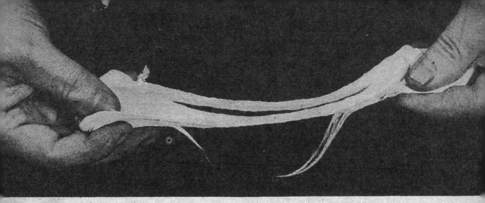

STRETCH IT, and it pulls like taffy. This curious substance is a by-product of research in silicone rubber, a heat-resisting synthetic used in sealing searchlight lenses and making gaskets for superchargers

Here Is Putty with a Bounce

Research in silicone rubber yields a strange by-product that may have its own uses.

EXCEPTIONAL resistance to heat characterizes silicone rubber, an entirely new synthetic product developed by General Electric research engineers. Rings of the material now replace asbestos to cushion the glass of naval searchlights and blinker signal lamps against the terrific shock of gunfire, materially reducing breakage. Gaskets of the same composition serve in superchargers for the B-29 Superfortresses that bomb Japan. These two war uses currently consume the entire output, but future household and industrial applications may include tires that will outlast a car, garden hose that can be left outdoors in heat or cold without damage, rubber gloves, and mountings for radio tubes.

Known for 50 years, chemicals called silicones have only recently been put to work. Hybrids between organic and inorganic substances, their ingredients are similar to sand and natural gas. A molecule of ordinary rubber has a "backbone" of carbon atoms, but a molecule of silicone rubber contains a more nearly indestructible spine of silicon and oxygen.

Besides silicone rubber, newly useful members of this chemical family include silicone oil, for hydraulic systems such as car brakes; and silicon plastics. A use remains to be found for the most curious silicone product discovered, which has been nicknamed "bouncing putty." The white substance can be pulled like taffy—but roll it into a sphere, and it bounces like rubber.

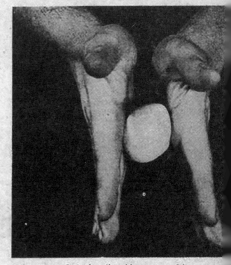

ROLL IT, and it handles like putty. Silicones re sent a cross between organic and inorganic substa

IT BOUNCES! Thrown on a floor or table, it rebo like a rubber ball. No use has yet been found f

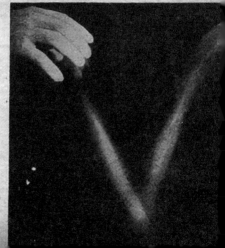

Silly Putty:
a visco-elastic liquid silicone with strange physical properties—
capable of
 floating in water
  or
 puddling on land,
  yet firm enough to bend
  and break.
"The Real Solid Liquid" the 1951 package announces.
Early ads say it can
 bounce like a rubber ball,
 be stretched like taffy,
 broken in two,
  or
 shaped into animals
  AND
   things!
That sounds more accurately like our love type.

When we are smooshed soupy, stretched to pieces, or waned of bouncy speech, we retreat into books by kindred creatures.

You suggested the two of us begin a book club for our *narrative/poetry/ emotional stomach-drop* reading collection. A genre I only discovered through you, a **limbic resonance** of like minds that led to my authorship. I read all of your favorite books. I read every book whisked from your limited but quizzically abundant shelf, and they are all lyrical and mysterious and so immediately stirring that I forget to breathe. I meet Annie Dillard and Mary Ruefle and Samantha Hunt and my mind has never felt lonesome since. And I recommend books to you and we take turns swapping books and thoughts on those books. We go to readings where we buy a single copy that the author inscribes jointly for us.

When I read a book first, I leave bookmarks of ephemera and scrap art tucked into pages. Your page markers are not so prepense. In your copy of *The God of Small Things* there is a receipt for peonies and lemons. I love that you let me scribble marginalia in your books like I do with my own. I mostly underline, then annotate with an informal coding system of ideograms that capture my reactions. I have a symbol for passages that remind me of you in some way. I realize now that the symbol looks like the double arches used to depict tiny birds flying far off in the distance. When I flip through old books and catch your symbol at the edges, I reread what once marked a close-up experience of you that has now become defamiliarized and it's as if the tiny bird is carrying the content away with it.

Sometimes I open one of your books that I have not yet read and find underlined bits or a few scrawled notes and it feels as close as I will ever

limbic resonance: the idea, as explained in *A General Theory of Love* (2000), that our brain chemistry and nervous systems are influenced by those physically near us. A mood contagion occurs whereby people in close contact attune, entering a shared emotional connection.

There is very little that anyone could say to clarify what happened next. Nothing that (in Mammachi's book) would separate Sex from Love. Or Needs from Feelings.

Except perhaps that no Watcher watched through Rahel's eyes. No one stared out of a window at the sea. Or a boat in the river. Or a passer-by in the mist in a hat.

Except perhaps that it was a little cold. A little wet. But very quiet. The Air.

But what was there to say?

Only that there were tears. Only that Quietness and Emptiness fitted together like stacked spoons. Only that there was a snuffling in the hollows at the base of a lovely throat. Only that a hard honey-coloured shoulder had a semi-circle of teethmarks on it. Only that they held each other close, long after it was over. Only that what they shared that night was not happiness, but hideous grief.

Only that once again they broke the Love Laws. That lay down who should be loved. And how. And how much.

On the roof of the abandoned factory, 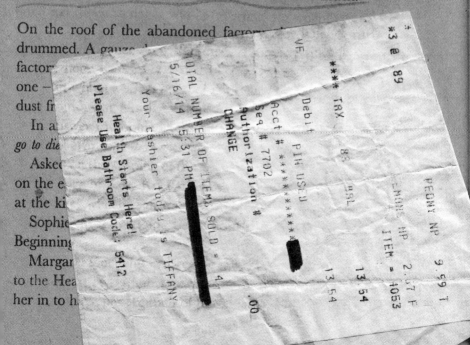 drummed. A gauze

factor

one —

dust fr

In a

go to die

Asked

on the e

at the ki

Sophie

Beginning

Margar

to the Hea

her in to h

BIRD BY BIRD   *Lamott*

MADNESS, RACK, AND HONEY   *Ruefle*

SWIMMING STUDIES   *Shapton*

THE ORCHID THIEF   *Orlean*

THE SONGS OF TREES   *Haskell*

SEA SICK   *Mitchell*

DEPT. OF SPECULATION   *Offill*

THE WAVES   *Woolf*

BLUETS   *Nelson*

SO MANY OLYMPIC EXERTIONS   *Chen*

OUTLINE   *Cusk*

TEACHING A STONE TO TALK   *Dillard*

FLIGHTS   *Tokarczuk*

MINE

BIRD BY BIRD   Lamott

PRIVATE PROPERTY   Ruefle

HOLD STILL   Mann

BRAIDING SWEETGRASS   Kimmerer

THE HIDDEN LIFE OF TREES   Wohlleben

THE SEAS   Hunt

GOD OF SMALL THINGS   Roy

TO THE LIGHTHOUSE   Woolf

AUTOBIOGRAPHY OF RED   Carson

TOO MUCH AND NOT THE MOOD   Chew-Bose

INTERIOR STATES   O'Gieblyn

PILGRIM AT TINKER CREEK   Dillard

HOME   Robinson

get to your inner workings. I paw at those pages, running my fingers across like they're braille, no, hieroglyphics, from some other peoples and time—here you were, now here I am. What bridge do we have but these words of the author? I cannot know if I would have underlined the same phrases since I cannot unsee the treads of your passing. I stare at the lines that do not speak to me and I sense you; I start to see thematic patterns, those patterns we each have that keep finding their way back to us through art. Our notes don't seem private enough for the other to resist lending their copy, but if I know you will be reading a book after me, sometimes I hesitate with my scribbles like I might hesitate before composing a text to you. Will my choice, of what of the whole to highlight, affirm or deny something of your perception of me? Maybe I like this unspoken opportunity to encourage a certain lean.

Without preface, you once texted an essay excerpted from a book, the conclusion of which read:

> I worry, once again, that my oblique approach has managed only to muddle things. I suppose I've been trying to suggest that subtlety is always a sign of mystery, and that our attitude toward the former is roughly commensurate to our tolerance for the latter . . . Anyone can pick up a bullhorn and make her intent clear to all, but to attempt something subtle is to step blindfolded into the unknown . . . Perhaps this is another way of saying that subtlety is a transaction of faith. The artist must have faith that the effects will be perceived in the way she intends; the reader must trust that what he detects beneath the surface of the text is not merely a figment of his imagination . . . Such leaps of faith can be motivated only by love—a love so fierce it is willing to subsist on morsels, taking bread crumbs for a path in the dark. And perhaps, in the end, it is love that allows us to endure these mysteries, to subsist on so little, believing that somewhere, beyond the darkness, exists another consciousness that is trying to reach us.

I was in disbelief. Still am. Was this coincidence, or proclamation being transmitted? I never know when to read between your lines.

The only times I have the fortune of reading your intended thoughts is in text exchanges. Your texts are always succinct edgy phrases, never in excess. Mine are verbose streams of consciousness. Neither of us like texting, but we have both personalized the medium.

We hardly use emojis with each other and always uncommon kinds, except the heart emoji. Never used in repetition, but laden heavier than forty hearts sent by another, its presence holds the utmost symbolism heralding back to its original inception. All of your texts hold such gravity or exist not at all.

leitmotif: a dominant or recurrent theme, idea, or object in a literary piece, performance, or person's life.

I dread when those three dots become never-sents. I am desperate to know what goes unsaid. When I am not with you but still in your head.

I love that time you randomly left me a voice message saying that you missed me, even though it had only been a day, because I missed you too.

When you are not with me, I am off and about living life and then often and sudden there comes something, maybe weighty or droll or staggering or something, anything at all will occur and I will wish you there to be sharing in the experience. I will be appreciating it more or differently because I am thinking of how you would appreciate it; I will be scrambling to imbibe as much of the moment as possible, more than my memory usually files, so that I might replay it for you later. I want to give it to you, I want you to have the highlight reel, I want you never deprived of the best life's got.

I amass those moments like a chipmunk stuffing food in its cheeks until we next speak. I keep from swallowing so they will be ready to access. They roll about on my tongue as I rehearse the retellings just right. Held there fresh to tell you first, or maybe to tell you only. I don't want the stories to rot in the wrong ears; I want them deposited in our germinating folklore.

I am dumbfounded by the differences in our memories. Whenever you recall something said by a friend during a mutually attended event— usually something anecdotal and phrased just so to be optimally engaging . . . I can confirm what is being recollected but would have never again been able to exhume it—mostly you retain facts while I can only grasp at feelings—accentuating how elseways two brains can be in writing their history. What a rounded tale we could weave if not told singly.

We are becoming keepers of one another's memories . . . shared experiences that only one of us will archive and be able to retrieve. We have no control over what we forget that the other will remember, and how, or if, it will get retold.

Once, you turned to me to ask about the last time you were scared, because I am around enough to know. I did know, it was two weeks prior. We had woken at 4:00 a.m. to cycle to the beach for a prework sunrise. On the way in the night, I looked back toward you before crossing an intersection, to make sure you were near, just as a car turned without signaling. I did not see it, but you gasped in terror. We won't remember that morning equally. I will remember the bewitching way the dawn then light changed the aura of the thrashing waves each moment of daybreak. And maybe you will remember something I missed entirely.

—

In medieval literature and occultism, there is what is known as the Green Language—*the language of the birds*. The name comes from a mythos that says the Roman god Mercury created the letters of the alphabet by watching the shapes cranes made as they flew. It referred to a secret and heavenly language housing perfect wisdom, with magical vocabulary and symbolic grammar, often using wordplay, alternative spellings, manipulations of letters, and the reordering of links between ideas. A language that bridges time and place so that any two people can communicate at transcendent depths. Michael A. Sells describes it as a language of unsaying wherein even when the heart of what is being communicated is never spoken; it is understood by those communicating.

We are far from fluency in Green Language, but I glimpse it most in the memories that overlap between us that layer and whorl time, the laughter following intimations, the shorthand written between the lines.

You are not only a master mimicker but a linguistic gymnast, a wizard of witticisms. You are epigrammatic. I love your rich use of vocabulary. I covet such diction. On one of your GRE study flashcards, I spot my name in a definition like I am the word's synecdoche, or its aqueduct between your language and **extradictionary**.

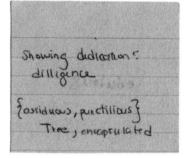

I come across the word *lethologica*—an inability to recollect the exact right word. I urge my brain to remember this word to compensate for all the words that stay lost around you, as a reminder that I don't always need a right word to define my experience.

I think of how Henry David Thoreau said that "the language of friendship is not words but meanings. It is an intelligence above language."

Even when we are talking,
we are exchanging so much more than words.

extradictionary: consisting not of words but of realities

Words are never enough.

Melophiles we are. One night my ears perk up by second 11 of Everything but the Girl's song "Mirrorball" playing off your phone. By second 18, I am hypnotized. Each time I hear it, I am lulled into a state of hazy contemplation—haunted and wistful. It simulates the visual effect of a mirror ball; time slows as dizzying illuminations surround.

Ever and anon you put it on while we wind down in dimmed light after loud days. With its spellbinding effects, it feels evanescent, so we must play it twice through. Once for me, once for you.

It played as I lay dripping in the living room that night of my birthday, evermore becoming a sonic replica of my love of you.

—

I made us a 1990s playlist that began with "Mirrorball" and ended with "Ice Cream" (coincidentally off an album called *Mirrorball*). It was only after being lovestruck that the nostalgic songs took on added profundity. How had I never noticed that almost all songs are love songs? Every verse of infinite verses holding equal truths about love's pangs.

—

THE ONE I LOVED IGNORED ME
AND CAUSED ME IN THE END TO MURDER MY BEST FRIEND
("MIRRORBALL" - EVERYTHING BUT THE GIRL)

IT'S A LONG WAY
DOWN TO THE PLACE WHERE WE STARTED FROM.
("ICE CREAM" - SARAH McLACHLAN)

Every encounter with a dingledodie is a gooey flowing talkfest, sometimes galloping across geographies or rooted in a place. Most socializing feels best consumed in bites then breaks. Before you, I didn't know another way to cut deep without being drained out. I am paced with you, sprinkles of many colored connections. I am used to the bond of words, but there is so much unspoken in how we bond. A closeness of bodily presence as much as mind. I love when we talk, but never with another have I also loved the rhythm of silences. The synergetic waves that can whirl in slow activities and a mellow speech. I wish I could forever be next to you.

Earlier on the day of my birthday house party, not yet knowing the cause but seeing my gloom, you take me to your Zumba class. You shriek and do a little jig when I agree to come. Maybe you're excited to have a visitor recast the routine, or to witness the merriment of your hammy instructor yelling "Twerk it!" as he spastically flounces around the gymnasium, squirting water on his face and carrying his own sparkle. Did you know how much that hour of sloppy energetic dance would help my body twerk out pain?

The earliest human civilizations participated in dance, well before the development of the written word. *Choreography* derives from the Greek words *choros* and *graphos*: dance-writing—the body as both pen and paper, words as prosodic motion. We swell and shrink, deepen and zoom. Our bodies require dance. It's an effervescence that yokes the inner and outer, the mind with body, my body with everything else thumping in rhythm to a music. It stimulates the kinesthetic, rational, musical, and emotional brain functions simultaneously. As one moves with others, brain pathways blur the barriers between the self and the other, resulting in a sense of symbiosis.

I join your friends for a night of dancing. You crave this form of socializing without having to drag people to your side. It matters to you, so it matters to me. I never go out dancing. I am a diffident dancer. As a child, my mother scolded me for not swinging my arms when I walked; I was robotic with my kineticism. I am abashed over my body's sensuality or lack thereof. I am confident in realms where my heart and mind are on display. On a dance floor, I can't distract from my physical insecurities; they come to represent all of me, a self seen only as a body.

It's true that dancing reveals another side of self. I am mesmerized by your dancing. I ache with an envy and awe by who you become. You are fiery, sexy, self-possessed. You love dancing and I love watching you dance. I love dancing too, but previously only alone in an empty room. But I have become breezier with age, making up for fluidity with zeal. Unaware of my reticence to the dance floor, that night you tell me that I am good, that you like my dancing. No one has ever told me that. And you mean it, repeating it several times since. It's a confidence that prevails in me. First to dance more with you, then to dance with others. Now I'm the one that requests nights out. Each time, my body subsuming to a synchrony formerly only my brain could canoe.

We are both drawn to the water. Both swimmers. On a hot-hot humid day we set out for a swim, one outdoor public pool after another out of order. We finally found a pool seven minutes before its evening closure. You had given up, but I insisted it would be worth it, begging the guards to allow us swift entry. We plunged, engulfed in blue. Its coolness quenched, satiating every incarnate and incorporeal droplet of our beings. Our eyes locked in agreeance: it was worth it; this deluge will go unmatched.

I now know the quintessence of blue.
I love that blue. Our blue.

The blue of *I* with *You* is *ours*, but an ophthalmologist would wager that our blue is not the same in me as you. We can see wavelengths between 390 and 700 nanometers. The wavelength intervals for each general color are broad. A person might call anything between 425 and 520 nanometers "blue," from where violet merges into blue all the way to where cyan becomes green.

Ludwig Wittgenstein talks about knowing blue and green, about the temerity we have in taking "a word to mean at one time the color known to everyone—and at another time the 'visual impression'" that one is witnessing in a moment through their own eyeballs. "The impression of color belongs only to *you*," he states. A word comes with a meaning, but maybe we also transform its meaning in our personal use. During the act of describing something, the descriptor is unfastened from the object. I might interpret a thing as blue that is not blue at all. I impose the blue on it, I hold the blue over it, but the thing is no more blue independent of me than it was before I called it so.

Blue has historically been considered a version of green. Color perception is linked to language. In many languages, there aren't separate terms for *green* and *blue*. Linguists use the portmanteau terms *grue* or *bleen* to describe when something greenish is approaching a blueness or vice versa. A marriage between the two. In cultures where there are separate terms for light and dark blue, people have been found to perceive varying blue hues with greater acuity. In cultures where there is no word for blue, people are less able to distinguish blue from green things.

We must have to expand to accommodate love of another human. A part of you now viscera, wedged in me so that I cannot compute without my neurons having to run along your form. It is as if I now have two hearts beating inside me, or as if half my heart is beating outside me inside you. My heart attempts to calibrate with your scares and sads and laughs and *whoas*. I love that I hurt when you hurt, worry your worries, can be absorbed in your quietude and laugh at what you find funny. I am innerved trying to cognize how you function, what your eyes see, what your mind mulls.

I am transported outside of bodily time-tracking through you. Hiccuping into our moments, everything else goes out of focus—like a wormhole opened and sucked us into an alternate dimension where we become submerged in water, dampening our ability to hear sounds or see the outside as more than a blue-green blob of putty. In a study by behavioral scientists measuring the physiological synchrony between partners versus strangers, surprisingly it was found that greater synchrony occurs between strangers than in preexisting relationships because those who habitually share physical space ultimately have less need to heighten their sensitivity to social cues: "Novelty represents a critical variable that induces alertness, excitement, and autonomic arousal, which might underlie greater **synchrony** observed between strangers . . . as a bid to establish social affiliation." I think our condition retains an unusual synchrony between lover and stranger, between forgetting and perceiving ourselves completely in the presence of the other. When I am with you, I nuzzle into a fogged space between us.

In an article about two close friends that drifted apart, one friend confides that what she misses most is "the third thing that came from the two of us. the alchemy of our minds and hearts and (dare i say?) souls in conversation. what she brought out in me and what i brought out in her, and how those things don't *exist* without our relationship." They go on to discuss how "all deep friendships generate something outside of themselves, some special and totally other third thing."

Our house can feel like a totem of that third thing, that blue-green blob. One day we buy a giant plastic container, gloves, stirring sticks, pH strips, cloth, other necessary ingredients to venture into the world of indigo dyeing. We each hold a handle of the container filled with the supplies, sitting back-to-back atop it during the subway ride home. We empty the living room of furniture and spread blue tarp across the floor; lying in the gulf we flap our limbs like snow angels. It was an elaborate undertaking from morning to late night. We made a playlist for the occasion, "Blue Dye Days," you called it. Any song with *indigo* or *blue* in its name was

synchrony: the observation of conscious and unconscious mirroring and adaption of physical movements and emotional states within the autonomic nervous system of people within physical proximity

considered. Outfitted with blue-bandana dust masks and blue athlewear, we churned fumy blue like witches over a cauldron, sprayed cloth in baths of blue, and breathed in chemical blue. With our soundtrack playing we truly were imbued with a halcyon blueness, blue staining not just our textiles but our floors, pots, and souls.

Color terminology helps to name and categorize multitudes into some sort of organized chaos. But to categorize is to separate and divide, to compartmentalize a totality into neat little boxes, like a watercolor palette. We can't paint the world without blending the boxes into obscurity. We can't paint the self without those water-smeared colors either.

We have a new housemate who is a grapheme-color synesthete. I ask her what color I am. I would have guessed blue. She says a dark green. She did not know me before I loved you; otherwise, I would have asked her if my color has changed. Has there been an admixture of our colors? Maybe I had the green all along and you are just an aberrant bleen or grue within me. A study found that the brain discards shade when recording memories, filing the kaleidoscopic into a linguistic prototypical. Maybe it doesn't matter of what color any of it is, only that we are dreaming and feeling, in color.

In Lois Lowry's *The Giver*, there is the gray world of Sameness and the colorful world of Elsewhere. Sameness is an oppressive place of absolute equality, only achieved through conformity to a homogeneous way of being. Elsewhere is that which is beyond the physical and figurative boundaries and knowledge of the community. When the protagonist is exposed to difference, he begins to see in color. The color comes with the ability to love, connect, and self-express, but also to be subjected to pain, tragedy, and incongruity. In the end, the protagonist escapes to Elsewhere, because even if it means enduring abjection, entering the uncharted also comes with freedom to be oneself and love everything that is else.

TITLE	ARTIST	ALBUM	US
♥ Mood Indigo	Annie Lennox	Nostalgia	m
♥ Indigo Blue	Jake Bugg	Hearts That...	m
♥ Indigo Home	Roo Panes	Little Giant	Tr
♥ Indigo	Milky Chan...	Sadnecessary	m
♥ Into The Ocean	Blue October	Foiled	T
♥ Deep Blue Sea	Grizzly Bear	Dark Was T...	m
♥ Deep Burn Blue	The Paper ...	On the Cor...	m
♥ Light Blue/Dark Blue	Nicco Direnzi	Installment ...	m
♥ Natural Blue	Julie Byrne	Not Even H...	m
♥ Dazzling Blue	Paul Simon	So Beautifu...	m
♥ Blue Mind	Alexi Murd...	Four Songs	T
♥ Bluebirds	Life of Dillon	Prologue	T
♥ Down The Big Road Blues	Lucinda Wil...	Car Wheels...	m
♥ Blue Ridge Mountains	Fleet Foxes	Fleet Foxes	m
♥ How Big, How Blue, How Beautiful	Florence + ...	How Big, H...	m
♥ When The Stars Go Blue	Ryan Adams	Gold	m
♥ Blue Moon	Billie Holiday	Solitude	m
♥ Blue Skies	Matt Woods	Blue Skies	T
♥ Goodbye Blue Sky	Ray LaMon...	Part Of The...	T
♥ Indescribably Blue	Elvis Presley	Elvis' Gold ...	m
♥ Blue Ain't Your Color	Keith Urban	Ripcord	m
♥ Blue in Green (feat. John Coltrane ...	Miles Davis...	Kind Of Blu...	m

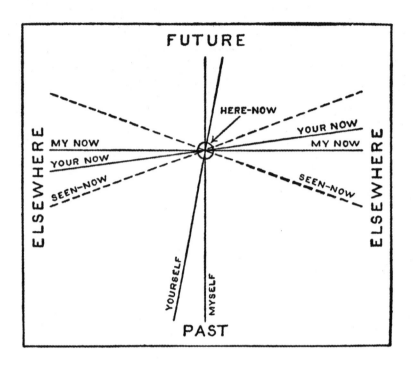

Else is a word of many meanings.

In Old English many "else" compounds came and went.
Went
elsewards
        to another place
elsewhen
        at another time

Yes, those *elsewhats elsewhithered elsewhere.*

Elsehow they exist   someplace,
                              anyplace
                              else.

They are a   something or someone
                           anything or anyone
                           else.

Those elses are the others—
they are not a this. they are of that.
not here. everywhere but here.

An adjective, an adverb, or as an *or else* phrase.
A phrase that leaves ambiguity about the finitude of a reality.

It is this OR ELSE *it is that.*

There is an *else of self* as well. The else that I become when in love.
The else I am with you, or for you. It is still me, but it wants to lap at a
common pace, to pause in front of a shared painting, to compromise not
to please but so that I might extend the self a little more into everything
that is else.

Else is a vague thing, place, person.

People are uncomfortable with the vague. The vague is without defined
edges to feel. It hasn't been prodded and measured, plotted and photo-
graphed in such a way that vacuums out the spooky unknowns. It is an
unpaved expanse free to be frequented at one's own risk

                                        or reward.

Vague comes from the Latin word **vagus**, which also means "wandering,
rambling, strolling." The human body contains a vagus nerve that sends
out impulses from the brain to every organ in the body. It connects the
brain to the heart and the gut. It lets the gut communicate how it feels
to the brain. It relates heart rate to breathing rate, which in turn affects
how our emotions and behaviors are regulated. It allows for response to

external stimuli like someone else's voice or presence. I imagine its sensory fibers like aerialists trapezing through my body and out to other bodies, every infestation of love animated through physical symptoms that say love is not only asomatous.
it is sentient, somatic,
beyond only brain or heart or gut
a geography without drawn boundary,
a vagueness of elses.

—

The only person I have ever known that reminds me even a little of you is my father. I am so much like him, but in the ways that we are not alike, you are—his cool genius and long listens and the way he stares into a person when they are speaking, pacifically supping the words before pausing to compose an elegant response.

I sit trying different batches of chocolate my father has made as part of his recent venture to become a bean-to-bar chocolate maker. Add it to the list of rigorous skills he has acquired for fun over the years: magic tricks, Greek, transcendental meditation, bread-making, fencing, ancient abacus . . .

What does it taste like?
Love? Some say love tastes like chocolate because chocolate releases "the love drug" phenylethylamine among other pleasure compounds. I love chocolate, but not a love like the love of you.

Love feels like
I am part of the world
in it
of it

What does it taste like?
Love? No, not love, my father is asking me what the chocolate tastes like. The chocolate tastes like chocolate. But that isn't what he is asking. He wants to know what else it tastes like. He is filling out a detailed form with notes on each chocolate sample based on my grading its intensity, texture, undertones, aftertaste, willingness to buy . . . I say they taste like October, like climbing a tree in a rainforest, like blue. *It tastes like blue?* He wants me to identify other foods that it tastes like besides chocolate, but I can't because the only ingredients in the samples are cacao beans and sugar. They vary in taste based on the bean's origin, how long it has been roasted, when it was tempered . . . even if other ingredients were used, my gustation would not be honed enough to identify such subtleties. So in the drought of specific words that connote the chocolate's flavor, I describe what the taste conjures in me.

I am an artist,
to taste something
I feel
then I see—
metaphors.
so many metaphors are used to write a book that tastes like us.

Not to get too meta-metaphorical, but perhaps the *you* in this book is no more than a manifestation of my love—maybe the real you is unprocessed cacao, and everything else turning it chocolate is me. This solipsistic take is irrefutable, but life appears to proceed alongside philosophical debate. And so I proceed in capturing through art the realest love I am capable of tasting.

Even Tomas eventually admits that there is something intangible that sets apart his true love for Tereza from love for the millionth part in other women usually only found in sex. He identifies a part of his brain as **poetic memory**, where "everything that charms or touches us, that makes our lives beautiful" is located and that no woman has been able to occupy since meeting Tereza. "Before he could start wondering what she would be like when they made love, he loved her . . . metaphors are dangerous. Love begins with a metaphor. Which is to say, love begins at the point when a woman enters her first word into our poetic memory."

I suppose these iterant metaphors, these leitmotifs reappearing on the page or in our life, are my mind's attempt to sort through the mud in search of meaning. It defaults to double entendre when confounded by the complexity. A peace comes in spotting a schema of one's **amor fati** and resigning to it. Carson says metaphors "give names to the nameless things." She says *eros* is often described with metaphors of flying and sprouting wings because "desire is a movement that carries yearning hearts from over here to over there, launching the mind on a story."

amor fati: the Latin phrase for "love of one's fate." An attitude wherein one chooses to see everything from the ugly to the beautiful happenings in one's life to be necessary; to not wish anything to be different but to accept one's reality.

Or, as Emily Jungmin Yoon writes, we are these flying "beast-lives of liminal spaces" that can only be threaded through metaphors, which are the "transportation, between absence and presence . . . what carries us, the slow consideration of what each other is, can be."

All year I wanted you to promise we'd be okay. I wanted the fight and resolution and a definitiveness, but you wouldn't give it to me. You refused to name an ambulating state that no language should translate.

Deleuze reflects on how humans are:

> Riddled with pointless talk, insane quantities of words and images. Stupidity's never blind or mute. So, it's not a problem of getting people to express themselves but of providing little gaps of solitude and silence in which they might eventually find something to say. Repressive forces don't stop people expressing themselves but rather force them to express themselves. What a relief to have nothing to say, the right to say nothing, because only then is there a chance of framing the rare, and even rarer, thing that might be worth saying.

Your silence infiltrated my character. Where I wanted agreeance on what would have been artificial consonance instead came rapt **hypocognition** that jimmied us into an else.

hypocognition: the inability to cognitively and linguistically communicate certain concepts because there are no appropriate words

Metaphor and movement nourish a mind famished by the dictionary's dearth. No word exists that encompasses the dimensionality of what you are to me. I cannot affix enough adjectives and adverbs to translate us into a sentence. We are not flat like type on a page or found in the apertures of letters.

Sometimes I don't feel like a metaphor . . . an inanimate object, a chunk of nature, blue- and green-ness . . .

I feel like

this

or this

or a hollow

or nothing and all things.

Sometimes my feelings circle around words before their meanings can be touched; sometimes they're of no use. I say I need words, and I do, but you showed me when to rest in speech's seams.

I have met so many people. So seldom do I meet a someone that can tickle that space between cerebrum and cranium where thinking and feeling commingle. You were my introduction into how wonder and novelty found in the familiar could initiate a far more sweeping love than what I once found in the foreign. I didn't realize how hungry I was for more challenge. I want to have to work hard to deserve the things I hold dear. And I have never worked harder to understand someone as I have worked to understand you. And I don't understand you. The closer I get, the more mysterious you appear.

Of all the recommendation forms, yours most moved me. It was a contrapuntal arcana that felt like sacred home. I have such a yearning to be granted full entry to your panorama—that stunning mental palace you've curated with fragments of time, image, and text intricately woven and strung elegantly like lace on stalactites. I glimpse it when you paraphrase a line from some essay or lecture or person you encountered long ago; when you share a memory that is altogether pithy, handsome, and gnarled; when I look at a corner of your bedroom where effortless strata gather: a MetroCard with Mary Ruefle's poem "Voyager" (*this life, already wasted / and strewn with / miracles?*), a resin-carved snuff bottle, a bird's vertebrae bone, Robert Hass stacked above Robert Moses stacked above a book on wilderness, a book on Mannahatta, an acorn in a gourd bowl, static scenes that scream in sparse photos taped overhead, a slip of paper where you've written "silence is a distinct occasion." The esoterism of your character scratches at me when I am exposed to things that you love that I don't find self-evident. The outliers erect a mood offbeat from my own, a mood absent from your public persona, like a corona I might only witness during total eclipses . . . eighteen months apart, scattered across continents, with special solar-filter glasses.

My hoarded warehouse can feel so inferior in comparison. As if I am a **magpie** too busy stockpiling tiny prisms and mirrored trinkets to pare down and polish what's precious. That's not really true. I know your view isn't superior to mine. Nor do you spend more time making it shine.

I used to trust that when I felt connection with someone, it must also be felt by them. But your certain rejection felt like an authoritative wisdom that negated mine. I presume you must know yourself and how we don't fit in a way I am unable to see. The muscle strengthened in childhood comes out, readily accepting your side. But what if it is you that doesn't see? What if we fit better than you are capable of experiencing or admitting? Our differing assessments could never be independently certified right or wrong. So I find myself forgetting my own glow. I hate how loving you can make everyone and everything else feel less sparkly. But that's how it sometimes feels to desire what I cannot own and admire what I cannot be. There are cases in life where we can trick ourselves into believing something or someone is ours, whether through the contract of marriage or receipt of purchase, that provides a false sense of eternal security. The difference with unrequited love is that I can never delude myself into thinking so.

You are the only person I have ever met that's felt brighter than me. I don't mean in a narrow category like IQ or EQ or some specific subject matter. I mean, you contrast me in such a way that you house infinite windows into unfamiliars. Tracking your daedal thought processes and piquant perspectives is like becoming beads on an Anatex's circuits. Ideas so strange I squirm about trying to reach the same conclusions. When you ask for advice, problems are framed to feel insurmountable. Our conversations are a constant puzzle I must solve. I actively search

---

magpie: one of the most intelligent animals. They pass the mirror test, which measures visual self-awareness. In European folklore, they are compulsive stealers of shiny objects for their nests. Science has since proven that though magpies are quite curious, they have no preference for particular objects.

for a piece of introspection or the phraseology that will fit with you. It awakens my brain, like all one hundred billion neurons zinging at once then finding a grace. Seraphic reward comes when it seems I have had a similar effect on you—the release that I feel when you reveal more, when words trickle then pour and in a flurry of connection you lose your cool and jig, laugh, cry, or feel. I love that you bring me to the edge of myself at the mystifying precipice of everything else.

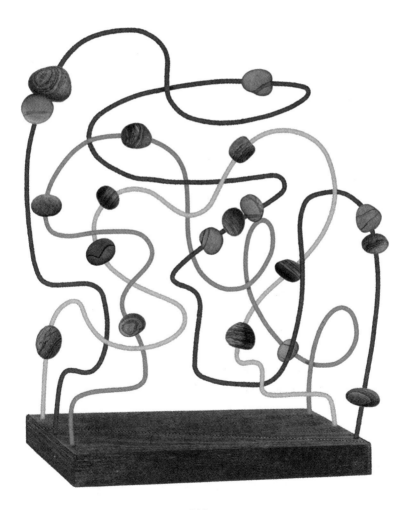

I could spend a lifetime trying to wring out and sip those drops.

Here is what I can provide no written evidence of: There is a presence to your silence that I cannot describe to anyone that explains why we are still here; why we stay despite how confusing the else is to onlookers and even to my own instincts that get scrambled amid competing indicators, creating momentary distrust and anxiety; why I fell in love with you in this way. The part of you that I will never be able to capture in this book is an overpowering radiation that you emit, so purely virtuous, kind, sensitive to suffering, devout to your own truth, a witnessing to life. It's this part that has its own language few can understand. I can write even less of what I am radiating in return, that language in me. But when I quiet enough to ask myself what you give me, it is the privilege of hearing you speak it and wanting to speak it back.

This book does not mirror the sensation of love.

I cannot say with certainty that any one thing I love about you would elicit similar wonderment if expressed by another person. To love someone totally leaves no room for comparison. Thus far there have been no near equivalents in my other relationships. With someone new, I must not search for your likeness as if there is a formula of one-to-one traits that could be added together to equal love. As with studying another language, to really converse naturally, one must stop trying to translate each word directly from the native tongue into the foreign and instead replete oneself with the foreign essence all the way from incepting thought to speech. The sensation that I once labeled "big love" might be universal in size but not in shape, which is uncannily the love of you and your presence's stain on me and this elseship that we have made.

I imagine this year, and for years onward, we are earning mirrored facets. With tiny spoons we scoop little bits—paper scraps, pebbles, dryer lint, zaps of intimacy . . . and each—solemn to delirious—comes as a fractal holding its own glint and angled like no other. It's a lengthy process of welding thousands of moments into a globular multiplex, a reflection of an entirely unique perspective of love, our rotating planet finding its own dancing light. It is this love refracting off us that dignifies the little things and big things one by one and all at once.

This book is not a mirror.

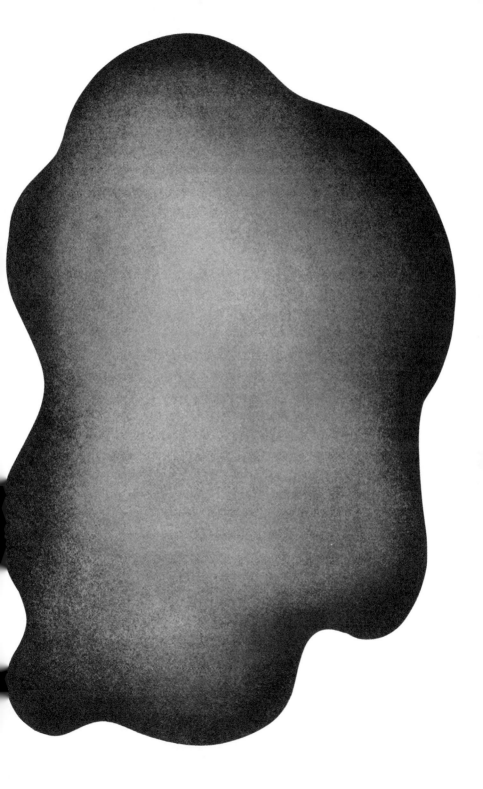

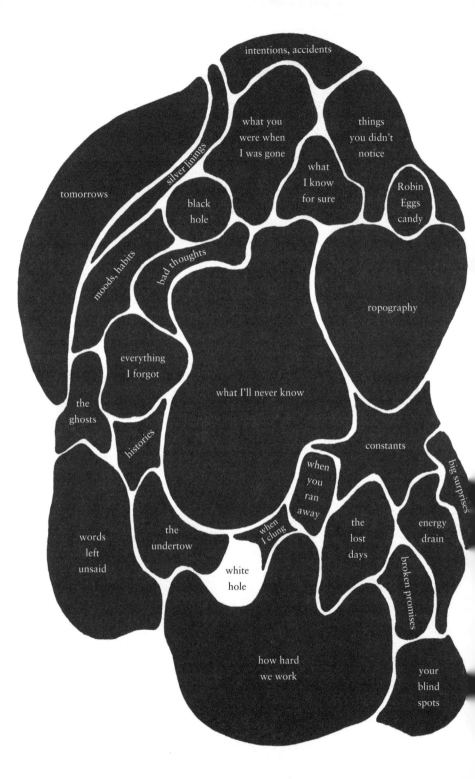

It's the beginnings of our mirror ~~ball~~ blob.

The best day of my crucible year was the day you finally said those three words back, 267 days after I said them to you. Because you say slowly. I, fast.

It was Friendsgiving weekend when we spontaneously went to my best place and scavenged along the shore for treasures and you found the best things and it became your best place too. You had packed tools, I had packed snacks. We rummaged and sifted, nibbled and giggled. It was a blip of sunshine and warm air between weeks of clouded windstruck winter. I watched as you experienced the exact same thrilling, gurgling love of a thing that identically exulted me, our waves undulating as one. Every moment of that day we overflowed joy, pronouncing it aloud and in our awakened faces. It whooshed and soared through us.

The last thing we find before heading back home is a large blueish-green glass demijohn. I spot its neck peeping out of the sandy bluff that erodes daily with the elements. I only need to gently pull it as the sediments around collapse and free its large bulbous body. I call out to you, holding up the glassy mass like our day's trophy. Twinkle-eyed, you hurry over to admire the bottle and assist with carefully zipping it into my backpack.

We walk on to the end of the beach; then you say *it*,
joining me in the in-between.

Unknowing of the day's occurrences, that evening a housemate remarked that we must have had the best day because we were both glowing.

We were.

Everglowing.

Will I grow too attached?
Will it hurt when you leave?
Will I long grieve?

Yes.
I exist on an earth you roam,
you are not a vague lineament waiting to be traced.
I cannot undo our meeting.
        And the memories,
                latch like barnacles on my lungs
                    so I can't breathe without reviving them.

One night the house did a Love Languages quiz. I still have the piece of paper where you and I scribbled our answers, but I no longer have the questions. The other side of the paper is a letter that was found tucked in a stooped copy of *Man Walks into a Room* by Nicole Krauss; it must have been in the book when we were grabbing for scrap paper and returned to its pages after the quiz was complete. I had not yet read it. I first read Krauss's more acclaimed book *The History of Love*. In it a man loves a woman but cannot stay with her and that love consumes his whole life. I am afraid of that becoming my story. In an exchange between the man and the woman, they speak of how each day they grow a bit happier and a bit sadder, but that those things don't cancel each other out. The woman asks, "Are you the happiest and saddest—right now that you've ever been?" Yes. The man replies, "Nothing makes me happier and nothing makes me sadder than you." I am never neutral in feeling with you. Our time either feels impossible or it feels perfect.

everglow: a slang term for the enduring feelings of sorrow and love, peace, or warmth experienced when thinking about something from the past that is no longer what it was. Coldplay wrote a song by the same name after hearing a surfer using it to mean "whether it's a loved one or a situation or a friend or a relationship that's finished, or someone's passed away . . . after you've been through the sadness of something, you also get this everglow."

Huby

① Ⓠ QUALITY TIME
② WORDS OF AFFIRM^n
③ ACTS OF SERVICE/ PHYSICAL TOUCH
④ RECEIVING IND

1. A	14. B	27. B
2. B	15. A	28. E
3. B	16. E	29. A
4. E	17. D	30. A
5. C	18. B	
6. B	19. D	
7. A	20. D	
8. A	21. D	
9. B	22. A	
10. A	23. D	
11. B	24. B	
12. E	25. B	
13. A	26. E	

A 9
B 9 10
C 1
D 5
E 5

13 12 11 10 9 8 7 6 5 4 3 2 1
C D B A B A A B C D B B A

26 25 24 23 22 21 20 19 18 17 16 15 14
E E B D A B D D B D B D E

3 2 1 6 5 4 9 8 7
E D C B A 10 6 D D E
27 28

Happy Birthday mi amor. This book was written
by Jonathan Safran Foer's wife, which is why I chose
it for you. There is no guarantee that you will like her
writing but I like to think that you can tell a lot
about a person by seeing who they have chosen to spend
the rest of their lives with. Therefore, chances are she is
a smart and able writer as well. I also think it would be
difficult to have a successful marriage unless both parties
were supportive of each other's work. I sometimes think
about what it would be like if I wasn't a fan of your music
but then again, it is such a big part of who you are that
many aspects of you would also have to be different and
then you wouldn't be the person I love. Anyway, I
hope you enjoy the book, if not, I will have to revise some
of my theories ☺ I love you Gordeeeeto.
                Happy 26th Birthday
                        ♡

I proceed to read *Man Walks into a Room*. The book is partially about love lost, of being alone in one's mind, the yearning for a loved one to fill the hole of unknown-ness: "Science is about sharing . . . The more carefully I can define something, the better I'm able to share it." A friend accuses me of writing this book to you. But what would that accomplish? No narrative could change what you want. Later the narrator wonders, "And what is a life . . . without a witness?" I think maybe love is about choosing who I want to witness me, who I know watches me in the way I want to be watched, and, maybe, even though I did not write this book for you, I am writing it in the way that I want you to understand me.

Why do I write the burning bits when I claimed at the beginning of this book to be writing only what I want to enshrine?

The things that hold us together can end up being the things that hold us back. Remembering and forgiving can be antithetical acts. What of this must I remember? What needs to be forgotten in order to let go and move on? Looking back is painful, not only in the recollection of painful things but also in the nostalgia of all things irrecoverable. I don't know what to do about memory. So much slips away, and the selective bits that protrude become distorted in revisits. I can too readily recall the worst moments as most of the best vanish. But as our story lengthens, as more happens that is so, so good and sometimes not, the less I want to forget any of it.

I want to remember all of me. I want to remember my wholeheartedness; a body that endured more than it thought it could, then more still; how hurt things that wanted to buckle into hate became catapults for self-evolution. I won't forget that I chose to turn the pain into love. I won't forget that the inner core of pain is from where mighty love can sprout.

I want to remember all of you too . . .

243

ANN TAYLOR LOFT - PETITE

SUNDAY NYT

YOUR HOOP EARRING + MY EARRINGS:

WORE BY YOU

BOUGHT WITH YOU

THE PRESENTATIONS

CUE CARDS

NOTHING BUT CHEESY POTATOES

SALT CELLARS

ABANDONED SELTZER BOTTLE CAPS

MYSTERY NYC UNDERGROUND

SOUR PATCH KIDS

SPRINKLE MOOD BOARD

AN ANIMAL OF NO NAME

OLD MAIL BOXES

PLASTIC STRAWS

FROM THE DUNE OF OUR PLACE (FIELD TRIP N°2)

UBER DRIVER FILING CABINET

LIGHTNING FROM WHEN YOUR SUBWAY CAR WAS STRUCK

88

HORSERADISH

MERMAID COST

EMBROIDERED RIBBONS

BRONX BOTANICAL GARDEN

CRAIGSLIST ANATOMY

REDDIT HOLES

ASBESTOS RETILING

REPLY ALL PODCAST (+ ▬▬▬ CRUSH)

A BANANA SUIT

SUPER DOPE CLOTHES

A CHAIN 50 DOLLARS

MY PLANT CALLED GEORGE

A REAL WINTER COAT

STRAY

WENHAM ICE EXPOR

DOUBLE-BAKE

STRAY NO BAK

FOIL GOLD STARS

FLOSS

RED PLANT + RED DOG

FACE MASKS

BOBBY F

THE BOSTON TRIP THAT NEVER WAS

DRIFTWOOD

WHITE ON GREEN POWERPOINT

LIVE EDGE WOOD + PETRIFIED WOOD

CHILI

MARSHMALLOWS

HURRICANES

SCUBA DIVING, TUBING, WET SUITS, SKIN

PINE CONES

ASTRONAUTS RAVING IN FOREST

FLOODS

YOUR WARP OVAL VA I KEEP FI WITH FLOW SPRIGS

"YOU CALLED ME" TWIN HAIR DYE/NAME CHANGES

ZIPLOCK TUCKED-IN BOOT, DAMP RAG TUCKED-IN SKIRT

YOUR INDOOR CLOGS THAT NEVER COME OFF AND SOMETIMES TURN INTO OUTSIDE CLOGS

WHITE FLAG

5

DENIM-SUNRISE-BOAT CRUISE-DANCE PAR

THE RUBBER PELICAN FOUND WHILE SEARCHING FOR FOUR-LEAF-CLOVERS

WALKING OUT OF A BROADWAY SHOW AT INTERMISSION

STRUNG MARIGOLDS

THAT NAN GOLDIN PHOTOGRAPH
HANGING ON YOUR WALL SINCE HIGH SCHOOL

SALLY MANN
BLAKE MILLS AMPLE HILLS

HOUSE OF
COLLECTION
(BELLY DANCERS' RESPONSE
TO 9/11)

MEERKATS

YOUR BABY MOUSE, MINE
WITH YOU ALWAYS
↓ + THE GREY, RED,
AND BLUE
ONE THAT
NEVER
MOVES

TIMBUKTU
BACKPACK

OUI/NON
T-SHIRT +
TATTOO

KAYAKS

OUROBOROS

* TALISMANS ☉ ☾ *

SERVATION SCHOOLS
AUGHTERHOUSES
ISONS
YMCA FBI RAIDS
HACKERS +
SALVATION ARMY

ORANGE
CATS

POINTY-
EARED
DOGS

TARGET EMPLOYEES
"DO
DOWN
DOG"

SMELL OF
LAVENDER + LINEN
DETERGENT

SOUND OF
GRINDING COFFEE
BEANS

HAND THROWN
POTTERY
THE SURPRISE YOU HATED + LOVED

PEPPERMINT TEA
MINT GUM

LEAVING
THE PARTY
BEFORE
ENTERING
THE GOAL TO
CRY MORE

NERD-RIMMED
COCKTAIL
MEZCAL   GLASS

CHARCOAL

DOW PANES

GREEN
HATS

MISMATCHED
SOCKS

ADDERALL
CANDIED SALMON

WORN-DOWN
HEELS

SALMON-COLORED TOWELS

THE STARS AT
THE BEACH HOUSE

M&Ms VS. SMARTIES

EGG CARTONS
"PERSONAL PAPERS"

FROM THE WONDER
↓ EMPORIUM

PUERTO RICAN
PAINTING

THE FAKE
ORANGE
BRANCH
YOU
HUNG
A ROSE
GOLD
CHRISTMAS
ORNAMENT ON.

LITTLE
WOMEN
ALCOTT

THESE
CHARMS
ON MY
BRACELET
PLUS 5 MORE

THOSE
MATCHING
NAUTILUSES
+ SOIL
PLANTED
SEA SHELLS

THE
HALF-HEART
BIRTHDAY
CAKE THAT BROKE
US

AMBER
MINERAL
ROCKS

MY ONE-EYED
DARUMA DOLL

SANDY
HOOK
DAY

WOODEN

PETERS
MARYS
2 ROSSES
GRETTA

ANIMAL
HEADS

DAY I CALLED OUT SICK, YOU WENT
THE DOCTOR, BROUGHT HOME
OKIES AND WE WATCHED THAT EPISODE

Once you handed me a fortune cookie and we both immediately agreed it was terrible:

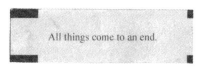

Those blue corners of the fortune slip are a suggestive extent rather than borders complete, liminal space between as possible exits off its auguring brink into elsewhere.

I want to prolong our ends. The mornings we ride the subway together toward work I skip 34th Street to exit at your 42nd Street stop just to hear those last few bits you tend to only say nearing an end.

You too seek ways to slow. You concoct a two-hour overland commute to be able to steep in spring. A walk from Park Slope into Gowanus to Carroll Gardens and Cobble Hill along Brooklyn Heights to Dumbo, hopping a slow ferry on the East River under bridges to Williamsburg over to Long Island City off at Murray Hill, shuffling through tunnels past bustle and steaming food carts up to where we part at Bryant Park. The fresh air and company rouses our day's start. I will always stay up too late, always awake too early, always skip the subway to walk longer with you. Those walks never feel long; we buoy outside time.

After a long hiatus, we return to our two-hour commute. We look up as we climb the stairs of *McShiny* to the empty upper deck just as it cruises under the Brooklyn Bridge.

Whoa.
Whoa.

The night I moved to New York, my mother drove over this same bridge and I saw this vantage point for the first time, only under a twilight with a glittery cityscape. I felt such ebullience for this place awaiting me. Awaiting is how it appears in perpetuum. No matter how many times I ride the subway, I unfailingly look up as we go over the bridge. Sometimes the train stalls here and it feels like the most welcomed moment to be frozen in time, looking out at the gasping openness that for me seems to hold all of possibility. When I choose to look up, I am choosing to hope that what might lie ahead will surfeit and captivate and keep me alive.

This time will end. I am not your queer life partner, your co-homeowner, your bestest friend. You are not mine. But I also must remember as I await future love, this love deserves to be lived. Maybe I needed to metabolize a first *love*-love this way—emically, in the cocoon of home, examining the reagents and reactions in me in slow motion—to begin to recognize its taste elsewhere. "It may be that friendship is nourished on observation and conversation, but love is born from and nourished on silent interpretation . . . The beloved expresses a possible world unknown to us . . . that must be deciphered." Unrequited, I could be most fully alone amid the tidal feelings, which mimicked the closest relationship I could recognize—that with my artist self. And just as was my process to every other meaningful confrontation with life, I wrote art out of the love in order to own it.

I see that Brooklyn Bridge and I love it, while forgetting I am on the Manhattan Bridge, which I cannot see. It is here that is leading me there, it is here that allows me to experience an awaiting love. I cannot diminish the necessity of this to get me to that.

The thing about looking up is what I see are not just the crowns of trees and concrete edifices and clouds. What I find, are birds. It took a while for me to notice that flocks of birds are not only concentrated in the exotic far faraways.

I have this vintage children's
hide-and-seek puzzle book
with a spread of birds.

It asks,

"Where is it?"

Where Is It?

31

Where is the love?

I know.
It's everywhere.

I make lists. Lists are how I unscramble life. How I break it down into digestible parts. How I make my art. How I make anything outside myself. I collect, compile, record, classify, index, enumerate. There isn't an obscure word for this. Someone who lists is a **lister**, or at its loftiest, a **cataloger**.

I have a list of words with unusually specific definitions.
I have a list of words that I never speak but I aspire to adopt.
I have a list of Latin words and phrases *splendidior* than in English.
And a list of venery, by animal. Like an *exaltation of larks*,
    a murmuration of starlings, or a *pandemonium of parrots*!
There's a list of recycling laws.
And another of eponymous laws.
I have lists of things to buy and to do.
A list of healthiest foods to eat and healthiest ways to eat them.
I have a list of   favorite artists.
                favorite trees.
                favorite songs.
A list of songs best sung at karaoke.
A list of   best websites.
                best podcasts.
                best friends.
A list of well-known people that I would befriend.
A list of skating rinks and swimming pools,
    of diners and rooftops and libraries to visit in the city.
Lists of potential road trips, day trips, professional and play trips.
A list of jobs I have had (thirty-six).
A list of things I don't know but want to learn (innumerable).
Lists ranking the languages, instruments, technical skills, sports,
    and hobbies I would take up if living was sempiternal.
I have a list of things I do not plan to do unless plan A fails.
    Insurance against listlessness.
When a list gets too long, I make it into a book.

I have a book of names, with twenty-six tiny yellow tabs to mark
    each letter of the alphabet.
I have a book of places to visit, sorted within 195 sections.
A book of dinner parties I have hosted.
A book of films and television shows and books with checkboxes
    to tick complete.
A book of art-project ideas unlikely to ever be ticked.
A book of passages and concepts, which I eventually transfer into
A box of forty-seven subject-based folders for things longer than a book.
I have a book of thoughts, with a list of thirty things to achieve in the
    year before my thirtieth (I copy this idea from you).
I have year lists in this same book.
And a seasonal list on my wall.
And a revolving twice-weekly list taped to the back of my phone.
And a daily list on my desk.
It seems like a lot, but it is just an attempt to map the mind's
    preoccupations, to remind of what matters, winnowing out
    trivial crowds of clutter to the core of myself.

And now there is this list.
By *this*, I suppose I could mean I have this list of lists.
But I actually mean this book. A list of loves. A list of all things
    I love of you, of us, of else.
No list is ever complete—things forgotten, missing, maybe added later
    or never.

We sit writing lists on New Year's Eve.

I reflect back on this year of elses. It was the longest year. The most
painfully manic. But it was also the most awakening, ways of being
mushrooming. I feel heavier now, maybe because of the birds inside, or
because you course through me, adding a few percentage points to the
55 percent of water my body contains, but it's a heaviness of the human

condition, of being, having, knowing more than heretofore. I can never go back to what I was. And I wouldn't want to. I try to think if there is anything I would have done differently, anything I could have wanted you to do differently.

You say that
if you could snap your fingers and feel the same way about me as I do for you,
you would.

I love this most ever of anything you've said. It makes me feel enough. The nature of love is absurd. It doesn't matter how much you consciously want something; you can't will yourself to feel what you don't. You can want something all the way and it still won't be enough to feel it all that way. I ask why you hadn't said that at the beginning of the crucible.

You allude to an unnatural self-restraint you occasionally impose around me: *Sometimes I feel myself wanting to pour into you, but I just can't . . . it's not safe.* You won't explain further. You always decide when a conversation point is done, regardless of my hope to keep going. I hate that you refuse to expatiate on behaviors that so bedevil me. At the end of those sentences I feel like I have been straitjacketed, like you are smothering my face with a pillow, like I am having a nightmare that requires me to run and scream for help but I am paralyzed. Depending on what was said and how you proceed, this feeling can last for several minutes to several days.

I think your restraint was about trying to regulate our pace with an opposing force. I was rowing us out into an open sea and you were trying to dock us to still shores.

Maybe this year you weren't ready to love me, or maybe you would have sooner had I not tried to name it. In reading about how everything can be made up of atoms when atoms are 99.9999999999999999999

99999999999999999999999999999999999999999999999 percent empty space, I learned that we are mostly whirling electronic waves with tiny-scopic cores. Solidity is a chimera. Every atom is constantly vibrating at an entirely unique frequency; no two electrons dance in step. When atoms meet, their dancing changes in response to nearby waves. Electrons then move between atoms to fill the empty spaces in the other's shells. Our waves are inseparable. I think. Quantum mechanics is abstruse. Even to physicists. So much so that they situate their work within the **uncertainty principle**, which says that nature is intrinsically fuzzy—nothing exists at a single point. And merely by attempting to measure or observe something we will necessarily change it. You can't approach an electron without affecting its course, and probably your own. It's like the ***butterfly effect***. The pioneer of the concept, Edward Lorenz, wrote that his evidence strongly supports the theory that "one flap of a sea gull's wings would be enough to alter the course of the weather forever." Similarly, philosopher Johann Gottlieb Fichte wrote "you could not remove a single grain of sand from its place without thereby . . . changing something throughout all parts of the immeasurable whole."

In this home, every particle of who we are, every action and inaction, inescapably coalesces into this blob, never to be reconstituted or filtered out. Your comment about safety makes me feel swindled out of the relationship we would have had if it were not for my love. What did we miss out on? How much closer could we have been? I am jealous of both your romantic and platonic relationships and how safe you feel in the roles you play within them. Our improvised interplay is punctured with perplexity. We steal our moments away from the real like an affair. There are so many conversations and experiences we aren't permitted together. But, during our New Year's Eve talk, we agree it is pointless

uncertainty principle/observer effect: In physics, Heisenberg's uncertainty principle states that neither the momentum or position of a particle can be precisely measured at the same time. The observer effect states the instrument or system for measuring a particle will disturb the particle's behavior.

fighting this fated state. Maybe I will never know the side friends and partners get of you. But no one in our lives will ever experience the elses of us. I have experienced your most pressurized and most compassionate self. I have seen how you react to conflict and confusion. I have watched you come to embrace the blob.

I tell you
if I could snap my fingers and make you feel the same about me as I do for you,
I wouldn't.

You are appalled by this statement. You say I am a fool, that of course I should wish for your love all the way back. I don't. Because I can't wish for you to love me in a different way without wishing you or me to be a different way. To love is to surrender. To be humbled by this phenomenon as grand as the universe of which we are just granular sand.

You were right that we are not normal. Normal people would not have subjected themselves to the wounding dissection of what they were to each other. They would have either carried on unevaluated or walked off to relationships of greater ease. We often faced friction, felt under threat, and had to ask ourselves and one another time and again, is it worth it? The abnormalcy was uncharted in us, so our path was labyrinthine; all to guide us was an intuitive sense to stay. It is not the bliss of youthful friendship. It is something else. Maybe effortful in its evolution but still actively growing, flooded in light, awake with an awareness of its fragility. It made us something not to be taken for granted or neglected. There is a feeling of preciousness, a sensitivity, a gentleness to us. I ripple in pride of you and me in this year. We are not normal, because we are **rarae aves**. We require a delicate balance of the elements. Luckily, we

---

rara avis: Latin for "rare bird" or "strange bird"; a person or thing that is nonpareil, one-of-a-kind, exceptional, uncommon, unusual, wondrous, extraordinary

have learned how to help things grow, we behold our obvolute moments, we are careful, patient, stalwart. We do not wither.

I type into Google "What comes after a crucible?" Google only knows one answer. "The Crucible" is the final grueling training event that recruits are required to complete in order to serve in the United States Marine Corps. Upon completion, recruits are awarded an Eagle, Globe, and Anchor emblem and officially become Marines. Inscribed on the emblem is a common Latin military motto: "Semper Fidelis" (Always Faithful).

Always faithful.
To each other and to ourselves.
What comes after the year of the crucible is
wild faith.
We are so small
birds flapping wings over oceans
specks of glitter
microscopic blue-green algae
seconds of time.
We are puny
miraculous
micromoments
stringing together infinite space.
We can't know what we are to the whole,
we can only have faith in ourselves.

So I wish nothing to have been different because this year was an indivisible multitudinous whole. Up close appearing of tiny sips, but from a distance one big gulp of love.

SARAH MANGUSO WROTE "MANY BIRD NAMES ARE ONOMATOPOETIC—THEY NAME THEMSELVES"

If I were Google answering the question "What is love?" I would report that once the feeling of love is awakened, the question need not be posed nor answered by the Internet. Because when one meets it, unequivocally it *is*. Not that *is* can be circumscribed. Only to say, one won't query its existence or the ability to identify it.

I used to think love fit neatly into dichotomous categories: platonic or sexual, friend or romantic, like a sister or a wife, in or out. But really when love flows through us, its expression in ourselves and toward the other is a combination of languages that reflects each individual's psyche and abilities. Love soaks our innards and forms a mold in the shape of us. Each experience of love is unreplicable and unfathomable in relation to another. *I. love. you.* in the way that is truest to me and *you. love. me.* in the way that is truest to you and together our love is free of outside definition, and is as saturated as we each are capable.

I know I have so much more life to live that will school me on the ways of love. My insights evolved marginally, then in one year synaptically exploded through the love of you. What would I say to younger-me asking about how love works when it is not about things but about human elses? I would say, did I know that I could love someone all the way and it still wouldn't be enough for them to love me all the same way back? Because us humans, we were built to feel all the feels, but not in unison, just all fully inside our own selves toward all of anything we might come to love upon. That love is a thing all on its own inside of me, all the way; even when it is about a someone else, it can still just be a thing, just a something else outside me being experienced as love inside me.

Unrequited is defined as a love unreturned. When I began writing, I sought to find gratitude in this box of love that would remain unchecked. But we are of an unlisted else with no box to be sat next to that will ever be checked complete. Our states are temporary, fluid, requited in one facet of one moment and then gone the next. But the love pumps from me through you and back as we rhapsodize and gambol in the other's aura. The *we* written of here has grown better than this year. Older in relation. I love you more now than then: in depth and scape. After years, the love isn't dulled. Still, I wooze. Still, I am struck by witnessing your lyricism—moments where my body feels like the stung peak of a wailing cry in disbelief over how much one person can be.

And now, each time we part, we hug so tightly close and long it becomes an exchange of strength. You will first lullaby, *I love you*, and I will whisper back, *I love you*, and we then tug tighter into one another before letting go.

I know that all the things I love about you are because of me. It's because of how I love myself that I am able to recognize the particularities within you. I know that loving you and all your things opened up a space for me to love others more deeply, and to keep loving all the everything elses of life too. The act of loving is greater than the act of being loved. And what are we here for if not to be love? and unite that love with all its forms that pulse around us. in you. in me. in the wind that will forever swirl between.

There is no guarantee for an eternal commitment to another. You cannot commit to anything different in the future that is more than what we are now, and maybe later we will be less or nothing. I miss you even when you're here, sometimes unbearably when you're not. Maybe I will be the one that leaves. There will come a day where the love and then its absence is too much and I will have to choose the love of my salvation over the love of us. But our elseship is about letting go of trying to control who you should be in relation to me and the story I told myself that didn't leave room for yours. I wanted so badly to write a story of us, as if one could ever write a story of two. I wanted to control every bit of it, but I have a wayward subject that won't be tamed. By subject, I don't mean just you but all of it. I can chase the words to make a fairy tale, but life is something else. It's an uncomfortable exercise in being in one's body and not escaping into the narrativizing of one's mind. Is this mindfulness? Is mindfulness actually equivalent to bodyfulness? I think this is elsewhere, and this else place is actually the most honest and real existence I can own, that nothing can be certain beyond this beat. So I wrote until the words reached their limit as I reached mine with this chapter. This book is the truth about how I experience love. That's it. It's mine. It's all I have. Whatever else there is or was or will be only exists in me through the ever-extending edges of that love.

notes

4   ***rhizomes and lines of flight:*** Gilles Deleuze and Félix Guattari, *On the Line*, trans. John Johnston (Cambridge, MA: MIT Press, 1983).

8   ***words shape stories:*** John Koenig, *The Dictionary of Obscure Sorrows* (New York: Simon & Schuster, 2021), thedictionaryofobscuresorrows.com/about.

9   ***teaching a boy to love:*** Carson McCullers, "A Tree. A Rock. A Cloud," *Harper's Bazaar*, November 1942.

24 ***grok:*** Robert A. Heinlein, *Stranger in a Strange Land* (New York: G. P. Putnam's Sons, 1961), 292.

27 ***GPS of love:*** Maria Popova, "Your Brain on Grief, Your Heart on Healing," *The Marginalian*, May 25, 2022.

28 ***inventing love:*** Tom Stoppard, *The Invention of Love* (London: Faber and Faber, 1998), 95.

48 ***lack:*** Angela Chen, *Ace: What Asexuality Reveals About Desire, Society, and the Meaning of Sex* (Boston: Beacon Press, 2020), 19.

57 ***dysfluent speech:*** Oliver Bloodstein and Nan Bernstein Ratner, *A Handbook on Stuttering*, 6th ed. (Boston: Cengage Learning, 2007).

58 ***iceberg analogy of stuttering:*** Joseph G. Sheehan, *Stuttering: Research and Therapy* (New York: Harper & Row, 1970), 13.

59 ***commanding ear:*** Italo Calvino, *Invisible Cities* (Boston: Mariner Books Classics, 1978), 135.

59 ***untranslated reservoir:*** Richard Kearney, "Translating Hospitality: A Narrative Task," in *Language and Phenomenology*, ed. Chad Engelland (New York: Routledge, 2021).

73 ***glitter chemistry:*** Caity Weaver, "What Is Glitter?" *The New York Times*, December 21, 2018, nytimes.com/2018/12/21/style/glitter-factory.html.

77   *overthinking person:* Stephen West, "Episode #160—The Creation of Meaning—
      Kierkegaard—Silence, Obedience and Joy," *Philosophize This!*, podcast audio,
      January 6, 2022, philosophizethis.org/podcast/episode-158-the-creation-of
      -meaning-nietzsche-the-ascetic-ideal-f8k5h-k8xfx.

102   *homosocial affairs:* Sadie Graham, "How Our Cultural Obsession with Platonic
      'Girlfriends' Sidelines Queer Women," *Vice*, August 6, 2018, vice.com/en
      /article/wjk45z/straight-girlfriends-queer-women.

103   *emotional orbits:* Kim Brooks, "I'm Having a Friendship Affair," *The Cut*,
      December 22, 2015, thecut.com/2015/12/friendship-affair-c-v-r.html.

103   *half-finished sentence:* Anne Carson, "The Glass Essay," in *Glass, Irony, and God*
      (New York: New Directions, 1994).

112   *Venn circle:* Ryan Yates, "You Need Help: You're in Love with a Straight Girl and
      You Want It to Stop," *Autostraddle*, February 28, 2018, autostraddle.com
      /in-love-with-a-straight-girl-advice-411180/.

117   *the millionth part:* Milan Kundera, *The Unbearable Lightness of Being*
      (Faber and Faber, 1985), 200.

117   *non-derivative desire:* Chen, *Ace*, 112.

117   *arousing spirit:* Vivian Gornick, *The Odd Woman and the City: A Memoir*
      (New York: Farrar, Straus and Giroux, 2015), 101.

129   *bittersweetness:* Anne Carson, *Eros the Bittersweet* (Dalkey Archive Press,
      2003), 16.

131   *whole and against a wide sky:* Rainer Maria Rilke, *Letters of Rainer Maria Rilke
      1892–1910* (New York: W. W. Norton, 1945), 57.

145   *limerence:* The term was coined by Dorothy Tennov in her 1979 book *Love and
      Limerence: The Experience of Being in Love*. First quote is by Tennov.
      Second is by Helen Fisher. Both referenced in: Valerie Frankel, "The Love
      Drug," *O, The Oprah Magazine*, September 2002.

148   *snow globes:* Nancy McMichael quoted in Lynn Ames, "The View From/Harrison;
      Collector of 6,000 Snow Domes Knows Kitsch From Priceless," *The New York
      Times*, December 7, 1997, nytimes.com/1997/12/07/nyregion/the-view-from
      -harrison-collector-of-6000-snow-domes-knows-kitsch-from-priceless.html.

157   *punctuation:* Rivka Galchen, *Atmospheric Disturbances: A Novel* (New York:
      Farrar, Straus and Giroux, 2008), 51.

173 *intentional convergence:* Andrew Sullivan, *Love Undetectable: Notes on Friendship, Sex, and Survival* (New York: Knopf Doubleday, 1999), 196.

176 *fully occupied:* Eileen Myles, *Inferno: A Poet's Novel* (OR Books, 2010), 192.

177 *seen/unseen:* Jordan Kisner, "Portraits of Women Coming Apart," *Atlantic*, December 2018.

187 *compromise:* Susan Sontag, *As Consciousness Is Harnessed to Flesh: Journals and Notebooks, 1964–1980* (New York: Picador, 2013), 74.

188 *micromoments:* Barbara Fredrickson, *Love 2.0: Creating Happiness and Health in Moments of Connection* (New York: Hudson Street Press, 2013), 30.

192 *peripersonal space:* Brian Blanchfield, *Proxies: Essays Near Knowing* (New York: Nightboat Books, 2016), 88.

193 *queering relationships:* Casey Tanner (@queersextherapy), "*Queerness has taught me not to place romantic/sexual partnerships on a pedestal,*" Instagram, February 10, 2022, instagram.com/p/CZzRy5XOGpd/.

206 *subtlety:* Meghan O'Gieblyn, "On Subtlety," *Longreads*, October 9, 2018, longreads.com/2018/10/09/on-subtlety/.

218 *owning color:* Ludwig Wittgenstein, *Philosophical Investigations* (West Sussex, UK: Wiley, 2010), 102.

219 *synchronous states:* Andrea Bizzego et al., "Strangers, Friends, and Lovers Show Different Physiological Synchrony in Different Emotional States," *Behavioral Sciences 10, no. 1* (December 22, 2019), ncbi.nlm.nih.gov/pmc/articles /PMC7017247/.

219 *the third thing:* Jennifer Senior, "It's Your Friends Who Break Your Heart," *Atlantic*, February 9, 2022, theatlantic.com/magazine/archive/2022/03/why -we-lose-friends-aging-happiness/621305/.

220 *forgetting shades of color:* Johns Hopkins University, "When the color we see isn't the color we remember," *ScienceDaily* (June 2, 2015), sciencedaily.com /releases/2015/06/150602125718.htm.

222 *elsewhere map:* Arthur Stanley Eddington, *The nature of the physical world* (New York: The Macmillan Company, 1928), 44.

225 *love as metaphor:* Kundera, *Unbearable Lightness*, 209.

226 *namelessness:* Carson, *Eros the Bittersweet*, 172–73.

227   **liminal lives:** Emily Jungmin Yoon, "What Carries Us," *Poetry*, April 2020.

227   **unsaying:** Gilles Deleuze, *Negotiations* (New York: Columbia University Press, 1995), 129.

240   **everglowing:** Daniel Kreps, "Hear Coldplay's Heartfelt New Ballad 'Everglow,'" *Rolling Stone*, November 26, 2015, rollingstone.com/music/music-news/hear-coldplays-heartfelt-new-ballad-everglow-66656/.

240   **happiest and saddest:** Nicole Krauss, *The History of Love: A Novel* (New York: W. W. Norton, 2006), 91.

243   **chosen witness:** Nicole Krauss, *Man Walks into a Room: A Novel* (New York: Knopf Doubleday, 2003), 105, 209.

248   **silent interpretation:** Gilles Deleuze, *Proust and Signs* (Minneapolis: University of Minnesota Press, 2014), 106.

250   **bird puzzle:** Demi Hitz, *Where Is It?* (New York: Doubleday & Company, Inc., 1979), 30–31.

257   **sea gull's wings:** Edward N. Lorenz, "The Predictability of Hydrodynamic Flow," *Transactions of the New York Academy of Sciences*, 2nd ser., 25, no. 4 (February 1963): 409–32.

257   **grain of sand:** Johann Gottlieb Fichte, tr. William Smith, *The Vocation of Man*, (London: John Chapman, 1848), 26.

acknowledgments

elseship was my very first attempt at long-form writing. Its fragments were cut up and rearranged across floors, printed out or opened on screens of those providing feedback, lost by some, and rejected by many industry folk. I wrote and rewrote, added and subtracted, left it and lived and returned over six years. Much debt is owed to my agent, Mina, for being safekeeper of these words. To my publisher, Mensah, for knowing where they belonged, and my editor, Cecilia, for loving and making them better—freckled light everywhere I'd missed.

Writing could be considered a form of healing, but publishing a book should not. Recovery is private, physical, and ongoing. Most of the people I owe that process to can be found blacked out within these pages, past and present dingledodies who have not read this book but know its contents well and remain my roman candles in the night.

Lastly, undying thanks to the *you* of this elseship that exists beyond these pages in everything we've traversed since. There will never be enough words for your worth.

TREE ABRAHAM is an Ottawa-born, Brooklyn-based writer, art director, and book designer. Her authorship experiments with collaged essay and mixed media visuals. She is also the author of the creative nonfiction book *Cyclettes* (a *New York Times* Editors' Choice).